How to Find and Identify Mammals

by
Gillie Muir and Pat Morris

Dedication

This book is dedicated to the memory of Derek W. Yalden (1940–2013), who gave commendable and much-appreciated service to the Society for over half a century as a member, Editor of its Journal and a most active President. His generous legacy paid for the production of this book in support of The Mammal Society's training programme.

Contents

		Page
	Introduction	1
Part 1	**Planning mammal surveys**	2
	Why conduct mammal surveys?	2
	The range of British mammals – what's out there?	3
	Where and when to conduct mammal surveys	5
	What to take on a mammal search	6
	Asking around	6
Part 2	**Making sightings**	7
	Small-sized mammals – head and body less than 130mm long	7
	Common shrew, pygmy shrew and water shrew (red-toothed shrews)	7
	Wood mouse, yellow-necked mouse, house mouse, harvest mouse and hazel dormouse	8
	Field vole and bank vole	10
	Medium-sized mammals – (Herbivores) head and body more than 130mm long	12
	Grey squirrel, red squirrel and edible dormouse	12
	Water vole, brown rat and black rat	13
	Mountain hare, brown hare and rabbit	14
	Large-sized mammals – (Herbivores) deer and wild boar	15
	Deer – red, sika, fallow, roe, muntjac and Chinese water deer	15
	Small-sized mammals – (Carnivores) less than about 40cm long	18
	Weasel and stoat	18
	Medium-sized mammals – (Carnivores) 30 to 60cm long	19
	Polecat, polecat-ferret, mink and pine marten	19
	Otter and mink	20
	Large-sized mammals – (Carnivores) over 60cm long	21
	Wildcat and feral cat	21
Part 3	**Identifying mammal calls**	22
Part 4	**Looking for signs**	23
	Arrival at the site	23
	Tracks, trails and tracking tunnels	25
	Tracks	26
	Insectivores and rodents	26
	Rabbits and hares	26
	Carnivores – fox, dog and cat	27
	Carnivores – mustelids	28
	Ungulates – deer, sheep and goats and wild boar	29
	Trails	30
	Droppings and latrines	31
	Droppings – shorter than 1cm	31
	Droppings – about 1cm or longer	31
	Herbivores	31
	Insectivores	32
	Carnivores	33
	Feeding signs	35
	Nibbled stalks of grass	35
	Gnawed or shattered hazel nuts	35
	Burrows	36
	Small burrows – less than 4cm diameter	36
	Small to medium-sized burrows – 4 to 8cm diameter	37
	Mole	37
	Water vole and brown rat	37
	Medium-sized burrows – 8 to 20cm diameter'	38
	Rabbit	38
	Large burrows – more than 20cm diameter	38
	Fox and badger	38
	Otter and mink	39
	Other types of hole	39

Contents

		Page
	Nests	40
	Red and grey squirrel	40
	Identification of some distinctive small mammal nests	41
	Harvest mouse	42
	Hazel dormouse	43
	Edible dormouse	43
	Hedgehog hibernation nests	43
	Corrugated iron sheets	44
	Bait stations for water shrews and dormice	44
	Hedgehog footprint tunnels	44
	Mammal identification from hairs	45
	Hair tubes	46
	DNA-based mammal identification (faeces or hair)	46
Part 5	**Recording dead mammals and parts of mammals**	47
	Road casualties	47
	Discarded glass bottles	48
	Owl pellets	49
	Cat kills	50
	Parts of mammals	51
Part 6	**Live trapping**	52
	Small mammal trapping	52
	Live trapping using Longworth traps amd plastic 'Trip Traps'	52
	Camera traps	53
	Nest boxes and nest tubes	53
	Submitting mammal records	54
	Sources of help confirming mammal records	55
	Summary	55
	Mammal Index	56
	References and further reading	57
Appendix 1	Health and safety	58
Appendix 2	Mammals and the Law	60
Appendix 3	British mammal species list with Latin names	63
Appendix 4	How to read a grid reference	64
Appendix 5	Key to the identification of small mammal skulls	66
Appendix 6	How to identify water shrew faeces	69
Appendix 7	Organisations with interests in mammal conservation	70
Form 1	General mammal recording form	71
Form 2	Site recording form	72
Form 3	Owl pellet recording form	73
Form 4	Longworth trapping recording form	74
	Recording Form Code Card	75
Field Note 1	**Cases where mammal recording has contributed to conservation**	2
Field Note 2	**Local questionnaire requesting local information on a species**	6
Field Note 3	**Recording small mammals under corrugated iron**	44
Field Note 4	**Recording mammal road kills**	47
Field Note 5	**Recording mammals in discarded bottles**	48
Field Note 6	**The Mammal Society Owl Pellet Survey**	50
Field Note 7	**Recorded mammal cat kills**	50
Field Note 8	**Recording small mammals in nest boxes**	53
Table 1	**Mammals (other than bats) occurring on mainland Britain and their usual habitats**	4
Table 2	**Mammal survey seasons – best times for success**	5
Table 3	**Identifying mammal calls**	22
Table 4	**Techniques for recording terrestrial British mammals**	24
Figure 1	**British small mammals exaggerating distinguishing features**	11

Introduction

Records of mammals are vitally important for their conservation; we can only protect a species effectively if we know where it occurs. Fortunately, mammal records can be collected in many ways: making a sighting, finding signs, hearing a call or even by smell. Their terrestrial habits also leave plenty of clues which indicate their presence. Learn how to recognise droppings, tracks, feeding remains and other signs and you will be able to identify the presence of the animals that made them. This manual aims to provide the knowledge and skills to help you do this.

Your records can be used to compile atlases, which provide a baseline against which changes in distribution can be monitored, at both a local and a national level. Inventories of mammals at specific sites are also needed to prevent inappropriate building developments in areas that are particularly important to mammals. Some species, such as the weasel, the mole and the pygmy shrew, are thought to be relatively common but are rarely seen. This is a dangerous situation because we may not be in a position to notice changes in their numbers or distribution.

Millions of distribution records now exist for animals in Britain. Currently about 65% are for birds, whereas mammals represent only 0.5%. The elusive and nocturnal habits of most wild mammals do not allow us to watch them as easily as many species of birds but this makes it very rewarding when we do catch a glimpse of one. Mammal observers who send in records can quickly make a significant contribution to the conservation of mammals by improving understanding of their distribution. We face a major challenge to put mammals on the map in the same way as it has been done for birds.

This manual was originally produced in 1997 to support the training element of The Mammal Society's 'Look Out for Mammals Project'. Since then, increased awareness and expertise have enabled the publication of several excellent county-based mammal distribution atlases. The aim is to help surveyors improve their mammal field craft and hence their chances of making sightings and finding signs of wild land mammals. Details are given on what to look for, where to look, how to examine the evidence and what to do with the information. Guidance is given to help surveyors distinguish particular groups of species which often prove difficult to identify. Bats, seals and cetaceans are considered in other texts and surveying the mammals covered by the UK Biodiversity Action Plan is dealt with in more detail in *UK BAP Mammals*, published by The Mammal Society.

When looking for field signs or carrying out any form of fieldwork your own safety should be paramount (see Appendix 1). You should also ensure that you are not disturbing mammals or their habitat. Many species are protected by law and disturbance can be an offence (see Appendix 2).

Lastly, please ensure that your records go further than your notebook. Always send them to the County Mammal Recorder or the survey organiser and help to increase our knowledge and understanding of the conservation needs of British mammals.

Part 1 Planning mammal surveys

Why conduct mammal surveys?

Mammal recording allows us to improve our knowledge and understanding of British mammals and take part in conservation activities at a local and national level. It is also interesting to know what species live locally and fun to go and find out. For some species it is a legal requirement to conduct surveys before any significant habitat changes take place (e.g. road widening).

Accurate information about distributions is essential for:

- species and habitat site protection. Key sites might include those supporting rare species (e.g. dormice) or a large variety of species
- monitoring changes in distributions of species such as those likely to be important to crops (e.g. deer and rabbits) and for those affected by disease (e.g. rabbits)
- indicating where future survey effort is required (e.g. areas with few records)
- indicating where reintroduction programmes may be desirable (e.g. past records)

The best way to collate information for the above tasks is to compile local and national atlases. Mammals are difficult to study and a comprehensive county atlas usually takes several years to create.

Do we need to record all wild mammals? Yes!

- **Abundant species**
  Species such as the field vole, which appear to be abundant, should be closely monitored for signs of decline to allow appropriate conservation action to be taken before it is too late. Field voles provide a major food resource for many predators. A change in their numbers or distribution would have a profound effect on a number of carnivores, owls and predatory birds.

  Other species may be increasing and affecting other mammals (e.g. mink predation on water voles) or competing for their food supply (e.g. grey squirrels vs red squirrels).

- **Species showing no change in status**
  Surveying these facilitates decisions about where conservation resources should be allocated.

- **Rare and endangered species**
  Surveying these enables conservation effort to be focused where it is needed (e.g. habitat management/protection).

Field Note 1: Cases where mammal recording has contributed to conservation

Importance of monitoring changes in range/abundance

1. A literature search of changes in the use of the word 'common' with reference to water vole abundance, led to early concern about the status of the water vole.
   Jefferies, D.J., Morris, P.A. and Mulleneux, J.E. (1989)

2. Subsequent surveys of the distribution of water voles funded by the Vincent Wildlife Trust alerted the conservation community to the reduction in water vole distribution, stimulated research and action to reverse the decline and supported the case for legal protection.
   Pat Morris

3. Badger sett records, held by badger groups, are used to supply information to local authorities and to ecological consultants working on building developments, highlighting the presence of badgers in the area, so extra care can be taken. There are over 300 cases per year. Presence of badgers can enable modifications to be made, avoiding damage to badger setts and influencing mitigation plans.
   Dave Williams, Chair of The Badger Trust

The range of British mammals – what's out there?

Britain's terrestrial species of mammal are listed in Appendix 3. They are relatively few in number compared with the diversity of mammal species on the other side of the English Channel and few compared with the number of bird species on the European mainland.

Our 'impoverished' mammal fauna can be largely explained by climatic changes, which occurred around 12,000 years ago. As temperatures rose at the end of the last ice age Britain's endemic mammal species arrived, having migrated north from southern Europe, with 'cold adapted' species arriving first. Stoat and mountain hare probably survived in the periglacial area of southern Britain, as they did in Ireland. As ice caps melted, sea levels rose, separating Britain from the rest of Europe. From then on, although the climate continued to warm up, the English Channel acted as a barrier preventing other terrestrial mammal species migrating north into Britain. Subsequently, many other species have been added to the British fauna by deliberate or accidental introductions.

If you aim to detect all of the species of mammal in a given area you must diversify your methods of detection and also search in every habitat type. In some cases tracking a mammal may involve a variety of search methods looking for, say, droppings, feeding remains and, perhaps, a fleeting glimpse of the animal itself. All this evidence adds up to a stronger indication that a given species is present.

Bats, seals and cetaceans (whales and dolphins) which require special techniques are considered elsewhere. See References and further reading.

More details about the history, ecology and distribution of British mammals are available in *Mammals of the British Isles* (Harris & Yalden 2008). See also References and further reading.

Table 1 **Mammals (other than bats) occurring on mainland Britain and their usual habitats**

Many species listed favour habitat diversity.

	Woodland	Riverside	Urban garden	Mountain moorland	Farmland	Grassland
Hedgehog	❏		❏		❏	❏
Mole	❏	❏	❏		❏	❏
Common shrew	❏		❏	❏	❏	❏
Pygmy shrew	❏		❏	❏	❏	❏
Water shrew	❏	❏			❏	
Rabbit	❏		❏	❏	❏	❏
Brown hare	❏				❏	❏
Mountain hare				❏		
Red squirrel	❏		❏			
Grey squirrel	❏		❏		❏	
Bank vole	❏		❏		❏	❏
Field vole			❏	❏	❏	❏
Water vole		❏				
Wood mouse	❏		❏		❏	❏
Yellow-necked mouse	❏		❏			
Harvest mouse		❏	❏		❏	❏
House mouse			❏		❏	
Brown rat		❏	❏		❏	❏
Black rat		Dock side only ❏	Buildings near ❏	dock side only ❏		
Hazel dormouse	❏					
Edible dormouse	❏		❏			
Fox	❏		❏	❏	❏	❏
Pine marten	❏			❏		
Stoat	❏			❏	❏	❏
Weasel	❏	❏			❏	❏
Polecat	❏	❏			❏	❏
Polecat-ferret				❏	❏	
Mink		❏			❏	
Badger	❏		❏	❏	❏	
Otter		❏				
Wildcat	❏			❏		
Red deer	❏			❏		❏
Sika deer	❏					
Fallow deer	❏				❏	
Roe deer	❏			❏	❏	❏
Muntjac	❏		❏		❏	❏
Chinese water deer	❏ & reed beds					
Wild Boar	❏				❏	
Number of species	**28**	**10**	**19**	**14**	**25**	**18**

Where and when to conduct mammal surveys

Mammals are elusive, but chance sightings occur with patience and luck. Knowing where best to look for the signs (e.g. under bridges for otter spraint) saves a lot of time, and notes on this are given later under the sections on signs. Certain habitats are favoured by particular species and it may be easier to locate signs in particular habitats (see Table 1). Although there is little point in spending considerable amounts of time looking for species that have never been recorded in an area, it is also worth keeping an open mind. It is particularly important to try to record mammals in areas that have been previously under-recorded. Checking discarded bottles, for example, is a particularly good method for collecting records in inaccessible, under-recorded locations such as mountainous landscapes where little trapping is likely to have been done in the past. For trapping and handling mammals there are legal and licensing implications, see Appendix 2.

Nocturnal mammals tend to be most active at dusk and dawn so these are the best times to be out looking for them. Ideally there should still be enough light to observe signs. At dawn, signs left overnight are more likely to be fresh. Use the signs mammals leave as clues to lead you to a particular point and to improve your chance of making a sighting. Table 2 gives a calendar for conducting surveys for sightings and signs.

Table 2 Mammal survey seasons – best times for success

Spring	Summer	Autumn	Winter
Hares, squirrels and other species show extra activity seeking mates and defending territories.	Courting adult hedgehogs can be heard 'puffing' and are easily spotted by searching open areas with a torch.	Some small mammals (bank vole, wood mouse, hazel dormouse and squirrels) accumulate nuts at feeding sites; the forager can be distinguished by characteristic teeth marks (see Feeding signs in Part 4).	Yellow-necked and wood mice often inhabit buildings in winter.
Hares are easier to see before the grass and crops grow tall.	Water vole latrines are produced from spring to summer.	Harvest mouse nests and squirrel dreys become more conspicuous as vegetation dies back.	Scarce food may force species that remain active in winter to feed in more open situations.
Shrews are often heard squeaking.	Edible dormice can be heard making calls.	Nests tend to disintegrate by early spring or after strong winds.	Snow will reveal footprints (see Table 4 in Part 4 for species that can be identified easily from tracks).
Otter and badger signs easier to find before vegetation grows up.	A good time for seeing young playful badgers.	Red and fallow deer can be seen and heard rutting.	
	Feeding areas, runs and latrines become more obvious as the animals are more active.	Relatively large populations of all species have dispersing young which results in more sightings in autumn.	
	Shorter nights and the need to find food for young force many species (e.g. fox and badger) to be active in daylight hours which may result in more sightings.	More hedgehogs are seen dead on roads.	

What to take on a mammal search

The equipment you need depends on the survey work being carried out, but certain items are worth keeping handy at all times when you are out and about.

1. Maps (how to take a grid reference: see Appendix 4) and a GPS app if possble.
2. Collecting containers such as plastic pots, boxes or bottles for droppings, bags for carcasses (if you want to examine these more carefully at home or keep a reference collection).
3. Disposable gloves for handling carcasses or droppings (see Appendix 1 on health and safety).
4. Appropriate recording forms (see Forms 1–4 at the back of this manual) and notebook.
5. Binoculars (in case you see a mammal in the distance, or want to look more closely at evidence in inaccessible places such as a water vole latrine on the other side of a river).
6. Mobile phone.
7. Hand lens.

Wear clothes of dark or muted colours and nothing that rustles or jangles. Once you are in sight of a mammal try not to move, but if you must, do it slowly. As most mammals have a keen sense of smell avoid wearing perfume or aftershave and try, if possible, to position yourself downwind of the animal.

Asking around

Much time can be saved by talking to local people whose daily lives may involve encounters with wild mammals, e.g. gamekeepers, foresters, farmers, anglers and pest controllers. It may be useful to have a list of species appropriate to the county with a list of some of the other names sometimes used. You may find it useful to circulate a recording form or questionnaire. Target certain sets of people, such as fishing clubs or horseriders, or use the local newspaper or radio station. Do not be put off by negative responses as mammals often go unnoticed.

Reports of species which are familiar to most people such as hedgehog, fox and badger can generally be taken at face value. Reports of other species such as dormouse and water vole may need following up. Stoat and weasel are often confused, as are mink and polecat. You need to enable the County Mammal Recorder to judge the competence of the observer if passing on records from other people. If you are in doubt about the validity of the record try to confirm it yourself by using the information you have been given to direct you to where the animal was seen to look for other evidence.

When making the record yourself try to be as precise as possible. 'Joe Bloggs saw a stoat on 3rd July 2013 at SN 123456' is more useful than 'J. Bloggs saw a stoat or weasel in summer 2013 near the hillfort'. Precision makes data analysis much easier and may be more useful for protecting a particularly important site from a damaging planning application.

Field Note 2: **Local questionnaire requesting local information on a species**

A water vole survey was carried out by Rob Strachan and the Wildlife Conservation Research Unit (WildCRU) by placing posters around Oxford city and inviting local people to a water vole survey training day.
Sixty attended and 75% of the forms were returned identifying five new water vole colonies.

Rob Strachan

Part 2 Making sightings

This section is divided into small mammals (head and body up to 130mm) and large mammals (head and body more than 130mm), which is further divided into herbivores and carnivores. Groups of species that can be difficult to distinguish are considered on the same page. Species that most people are familiar with, such as fox and badger, are not discussed. The relative size of animals is indicated on each page and where necessary a picture of a standard object has been included to illustrate this. Drawings show only adults; there may be considerable variation within a species due to differences in age and sex.

Small-sized mammals – head and body less than 130mm long

Common shrew, pygmy shrew and water shrew (red-toothed shrews)

The water shrew can be distinguished from the other two species by its larger size and its habit of diving and swimming as well as by the features mentioned below. White-toothed shrews occur on the Isles of Scilly and the Channel Islands, but not on mainland Britain.

APPROXIMATE ACTUAL SIZE

Features	Common shrew	Pygmy shrew	Water shrew
Coat colour	Dark brown – three tone coat: dark back, paler sides and paler still underside	Paler brown – two-tone coat: dark back and pale underside	Black fur on back and silvery grey underside with sharp demarkation in adults, sometimes all black
Tail	A few stiff hairs under tail. Tail about half length of head and body	A proportionately longer, thicker and more hairy tail, at least three-quarters the length of head and body	Prominent keel of stiff silvery hair under tail like a rudder
Feet	Short hairs fringing toes	Short hairs fringing toes	Prominent stiff silvery hairs fringing toes
Head	Not particularly domed	Domed	Not particularly domed
Eye patch	No eye patch	No eye patch	Often with white patch above eye
Distinctive features			Larger with a habit of swimming and diving

Wood mouse, yellow-necked mouse, house mouse, harvest mouse and hazel dormouse

Adult yellow-necked mice are 1.5 times bigger than adult wood mice, but can only be distinguished for sure by examining the underside of the neck. Yellow-necked mice have an unbroken yellow band passing across the chest, linking the forelegs, whereas wood mice have a white chest usually with a longitudinal orange streak or spot. Mind your fingers, mice bite! Yellow-necked mice tend to be more exuberant and bite more readily (and harder) than wood mice. Young house mice and wood mice are rather similar, although house mice are always grey-brown with smaller eyes and ears and a thicker hairless tail. Adult wood mice have a white underside and a brown back, whereas house mice are all one colour although slightly darker on top. House mice have greasy fur and smell strongly. The hazel dormouse is the only small mammal with a thick furry tail (and almost uniform orange-yellow fur).

Features	Wood mouse	Yellow-necked mouse	Harvest mouse	House mouse	Hazel dormouse
Chest marks	White chest and usually a longitudinal orange streak between forelegs	Unbroken yellow band passing across the chest, joining the forelegs	None	None	None
Colour of back	Reddish-brown	Reddish-brown	Golden-brown	Greyish-brown	Adults orange-yellow. Juveniles greyer
Colour of underside	Pale grey/white	Very pale grey/white	Very pale grey/white	Greyish-brown	Yellow, white on throat
Ear size	Large (15–17mm)	Large (16–18mm)	Small (7–9mm)	Medium (12–15mm)	Medium (about 12mm)
Tail	Fur black on top	Fur black on top	Prehensile, brown/pink all over with some fur	Brown/pink all over with little fur	Bushy
Other distinctive features			Smaller than other British mice with blunt, vole-like muzzle	Greasy fur and strong 'mouse' smell	Short muzzle, long whiskers, prominent black eyes

Viewing Tips — To attract small mammals try regularly putting out seeds, raisins or chocolate drops for rodents, and dried mealworms or casters (fly pupae available from fishing shops) for shrews, at an observation point, such as in front of a window or on a mammal table. Put the food out just before dusk to prevent it being taken by birds. Cover the area (using a tunnel of wire mesh) if small mammals are at risk of being taken by predators.

Field vole and bank vole

Features	Bank vole	Field vole	Orkney/Guernsey vole
Colour of back	Reddish brown	Yellowish or greyish brown	Yellowish or greyish brown
Tail length as % of head and body	50%	30%	30%
Tail colour	Dark on top, white below	Pale brown all over	Pale brown all over
Ears	Prominent	Hardly visible	Prominent

BANK VOLE

FIELD VOLE

APPROXIMATE ACTUAL SIZE

Figure 1 British small mammals exaggerating distinguishing features

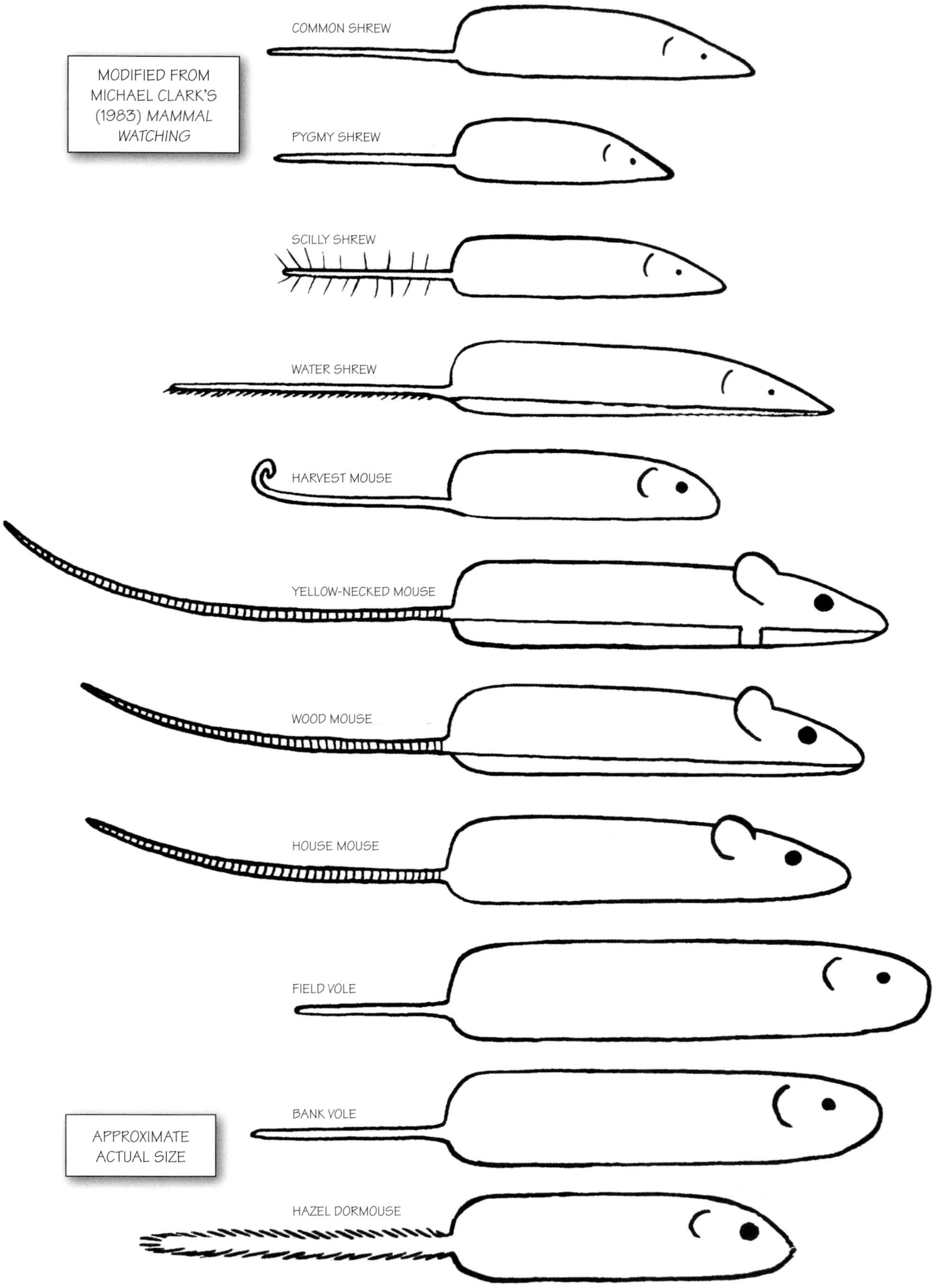

MODIFIED FROM MICHAEL CLARK'S (1983) MAMMAL WATCHING

COMMON SHREW

PYGMY SHREW

SCILLY SHREW

WATER SHREW

HARVEST MOUSE

YELLOW-NECKED MOUSE

WOOD MOUSE

HOUSE MOUSE

FIELD VOLE

BANK VOLE

APPROXIMATE ACTUAL SIZE

HAZEL DORMOUSE

Medium-sized mammals – (Herbivores) head and body more than 130mm long

Grey squirrel, red squirrel and edible dormouse

An adult edible dormouse is actually hard to confuse with a hazel dormouse! It is twice the size and grey. It is more easily confused with a grey squirrel because of its colour and bushy tail. The tail of the edible dormouse is, however, dark brown whereas the grey squirrel's is khaki with a white fringe.

Viewing Tips

In urban settings both red and grey squirrels often become tame and will even feed from the hand. In rural surroundings, however, both species may remain shy. Greys tend to spend more time on the ground whereas reds spend nearly all their time in the tree canopy and are harder to see. Red squirrels are probably best spotted by walking slowly along forest paths looking up into the canopy. In winter reds may become tinged with grey but develop characteristic ear tufts which distinguish them from greys. In summer the grey squirrel can have very brown feet and flanks.

Features	Hazel dormouse	Edible dormouse	Grey squirrel	Red squirrel
Tail	Bushy – orange-brown	Very bushy dark brown or grey tail with all the hairs a single colour	Tail hairs are banded in brown and black with white tips creating a multi-coloured tail	Bushy and red (all one colour) and occasionally very dark. Pale in summer
Coat	Orange-yellow	Grey	Grey – often with brown tinge on back, especially in summer. Black ones common in Bedford/Cambridge area	Reddish-brown (grey tinge in winter). Can be very dark but not black

RELATIVE SIZE OF A TIN OF BEANS

EDIBLE DORMOUSE

EAR TUFTS OF RED SQUIRREL IN WINTER

GREY SQUIRREL

RED SQUIRREL

Water vole, brown rat and black rat

Viewing Tips — Water voles can be spotted by ambling slowly along a suitable canal or river. Do not automatically assume that a swimming rat-sized animal is a water vole as the brown rat is also semi-aquatic. They can be observed from a vantage point such as a bridge. Once you have spotted an animal, move only when it is under water, to reduce the distance between you and the animal when it reappears.

Features	Water vole	Brown rat	Black rat (almost extinct now)
Coat colour	Dark brown (may be black, especially in northern Scotland)	Grey-brown – grey belly	Black (longer, sleeker fur than brown rat) can sometimes be grey-brown
Muzzle	Blunt and vole-like	Pointed	Very pointed
Tail	Slightly furry and much shorter than the body – about 60% of body length	Hairless and 10% shorter than the body	Hairless and up to 20% longer than body
Ears	Small, very hard to see	Large	Pink and very large
Sound on entering water	A characteristic 'plop'	No sound	Doesn't enter water
Occurrence in buildings	Not in buildings	Often in buildings	Mainly in buildings

WATER VOLE

BLACK RAT

BROWN RAT

RELATIVE SIZE OF A TIN OF BEANS

Mountain hare, brown hare and rabbit

Viewing Tips Scrutinise any short crops such as winter wheat. Go early in the day and use binoculars or a telescope to inspect fields. Brown hares have a long loping gait, rabbits scurry and hop. Do the same in heather moorland to improve the chances of seeing mountain hares. These species tend to be most active at dusk and dawn.

Features	Mountain hare	Brown hare	Rabbit
Ear length	Midway between brown hare and rabbit	Long – about twice the length of the head	Short – about the same length as the head
Ear tip colour	Black	Black	Brown
Tail colour	All white	Black on top	Dark on top
Eyes	Brown	Golden staring eyes	Brown
Body colour	Grey (or white in winter)	Grizzled, orange-brown flanks	Greyish-brown

MOUNTAIN HARE

BROWN HARE

RABBIT

RELATIVE SIZE OF A TIN OF BEANS

How to Find and Identify Mammals
The Mammal Society

Large-sized mammals – (Herbivores) deer and wild boar

Deer – red, sika, fallow, roe, muntjac and Chinese water deer

Features	Red	Sika	Fallow	Roe	Muntjac	Chinese water deer
Rump	Buff	Heart-shaped white with black upper border flared out when alarmed	Heart-shaped white with horseshoe-shaped black border	Cream-white which can be flared when alarmed	Dark	Dark
Tail	Ginger buff	White (with thin vertical black streak)	Black and comparatively long	No visible tail. In winter female has a tuft of long hair between back legs	When alarmed, tail held vertical to show white underside	Stumpy – never held erect as in muntjac
Seasonal coat change	Coat changes from grey-brown in winter to red-brown in summer	Distinct spots in summer on brown	Distinct spots in summer. Sometimes all dark when the spots are not visible	Summer – chestnut. Winter – greyish brown	Chestnut brown in summer, darker brown in winter	None
Antlers of mature male	Large branched	Typically more than 4 points per antler	Upper part of antler broad and flattened	Small branches typically less than 4 points	Single spikes pointing backwards with or without very small brow tine usually less than 10cm	None
Other distinguishing features		Grey-brown black in winter, no spots	Colour variable ranging from white to black but mostly brown with spots	Black nose and white chin	Males have tusks (upper canine teeth) protruding 2cm below lip	Males have long curved tusks (upper canine teeth) protruding up to 7cm below lower jaw
Females	Smaller than males and no antlers					

Small-sized mammals – (Carnivores) less than about 40cm long

Weasel and stoat

Weasels and stoats are both smaller than other British carnivores, and are the only mustelids with a red/brown back and white underside. They are often seen during the day.

Stoats, even young ones, have a black tip to the tail (the tip being the last 20%) and this feature distinguishes them from all other British mammals, including weasels.

Features	Weasel	Stoat
Tail colour	All red-brown	Black tip
Flank colour division	Wavy	Straight (wavy in Irish stoats)
Underside	White	Creamy or pale yellow
Other	Brown spot either side of throat	Throat uniform, no spots
Seasonal coat change	None	May sometimes change to white in winter, but retains black tail tip

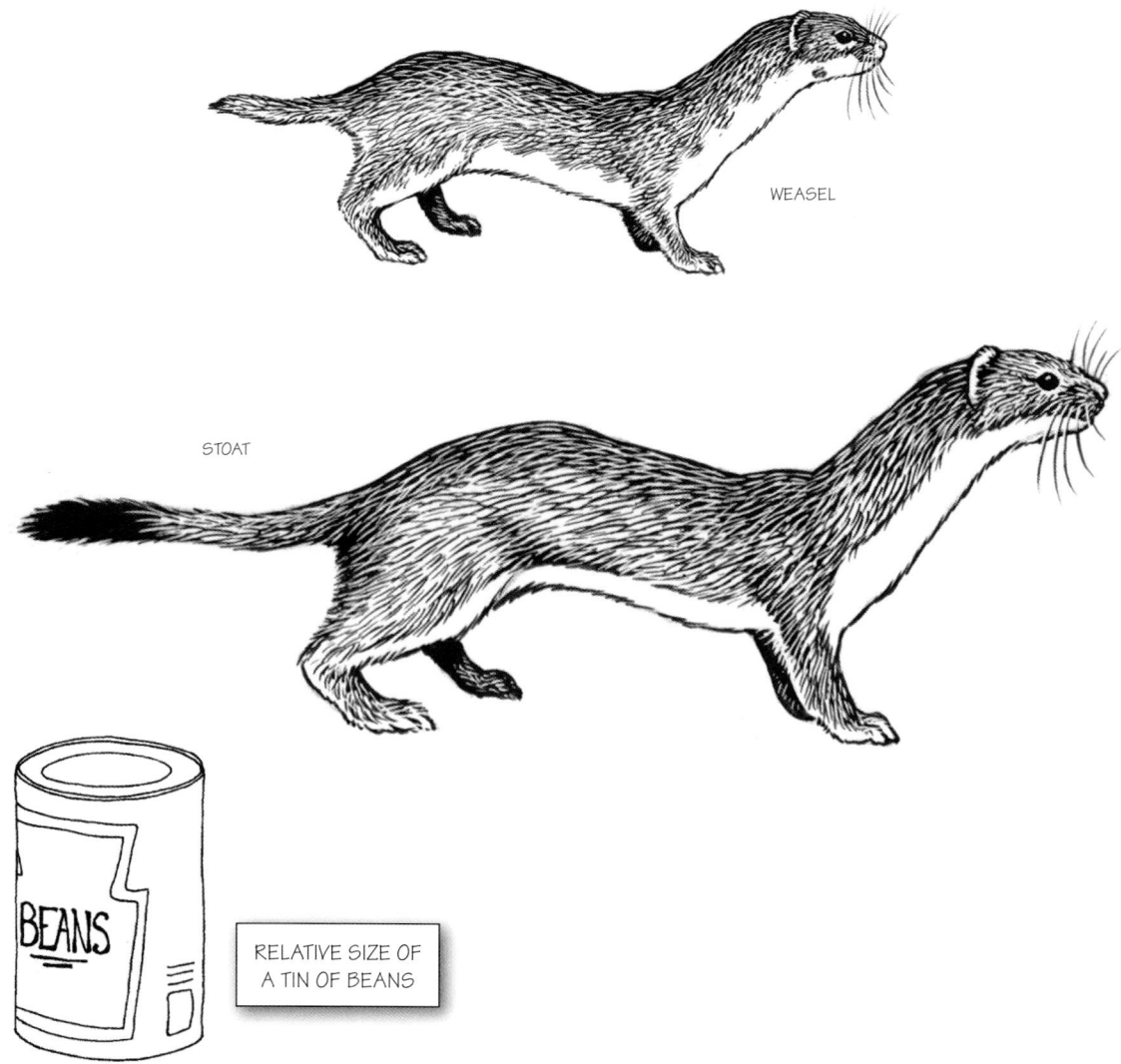

WEASEL

STOAT

RELATIVE SIZE OF A TIN OF BEANS

Medium-sized mammals – (Carnivores) 30 to 60cm long

Polecat, polecat-ferret, mink and pine marten

All four species are larger than stoats and darker brown (although polecat-ferrets may vary from albino to dark brown and are sometimes almost indistinguishable from wild polecats). They are also more nocturnal and harder to observe. Compared to a domestic cat all have short legs and a thick tail. The ears of the pine marten are slightly more conspicuous than the polecat, polecat-ferret and mink and it has a slightly longer and bushier tail. The pine marten is the only one of these species which is often seen in trees. Apart from direct sightings most records are from road casualties.

Features	Polecat	Polecat-ferret	Mink	Pine marten
Face	White face band	White face band (usually less distinct than polecat)	All brown except a small white patch under the chin	Dark brown
Chest	Blackish	Dark brown – may have small white patches	Dark brown	Creamy white
Coat colour	Blackish with pale underfur	Blackish with pale underfur often paler than polecats and with more colour variation	Usually dark brown	Dark brown

RELATIVE SIZE OF A TIN OF BEANS

Medium-sized mammals – (Carnivores) 30 to 60cm long
Otter and mink

Features	Otter	Mink
Coat colour	Mid-brown	Chocolate brown/black
Tail	Long, tapering, muscular and sleek	Cylindrical and fluffy
Face	Broad muzzle	Pointed muzzle
Size	Larger than cat	Smaller than cat
Other features	Creates bow wave when swimming	No bow wave created

Viewing Tips An adult otter is much larger than a domestic cat whereas mink are smaller. In the water an otter can be distinguished from a mink and aquatic rodents by its large size, flattened head and the distinctive V-shaped wake.

RELATIVE SIZE OF A TIN OF BEANS

OTTER

OTTER HEAD (NOT TO SCALE)

MINK

MINK HEAD (NOT TO SCALE)

OTTER SWIMMING

MINK SWIMMING

WATER VOLE SWIMMING

Large-sized mammals – (Carnivores) over 60cm long
Wildcat and feral cat

Wildcats produce fertile hybrids with domestic cats. There is therefore, great variation in the appearance of these cats in the wild. Specimens like the wildcat illustrated below still exist and should be carefully recorded.

Features	Wildcat	Feral cat
Tail	Thick, bushy and blunt with a black tip	Tapering tail
Colour	Tabby with flank stripes	Various
Other	Unlikely to be seen except in Scotland	Widespread including Scotland

WILDCAT

FERAL CAT

RELATIVE SIZE OF A TIN OF BEANS

Part 3 Identifying mammal calls

Table 3   Identifying mammal calls

Species	Description of calls and commonly made sounds	Season
Hedgehog	Puffing when courting	Summer
Shrew	High pitched, almost ultrasonic squeaks	
Rabbit	Scream when attacked by a predator	
Yellow-necked mouse	Squeak vociferously, especially when handled	
Edible dormouse	Calls, churring or wheezing sound made from up trees	
Grey squirrel	Churring noises in trees	
Fox	Short barks, higher pitched than a dog. Also screams	Early in the year
Badger	Cubs may make a short high-pitched yelp when playing	Spring
Otter	Whistle is made as a contact call. 'Hah!' is an anxiety call	
Wildcat	Hiss when disturbed	
Roe deer	Short alarm bark	
Red deer	Stags roar at adversaries in rutting season. Dominant hinds produce alarm bark all year	Autumn
Sika deer	Stags make a variety of sounds, including a distinctive whistle and a sound like a squeaky hinge	
Fallow deer	Bucks make a loud gurgling belching noise and short alarm bark in rutting season	Autumn
Muntjac	Loud single bark when alarmed, when does are in season or have just given birth	
Chinese water deer	Loud dog-like bark	

Part 4 Looking for signs

Mammals (except bats) tend to spend more of their time on the ground than birds and often communicate, or mark their territory, by leaving droppings or by scent marking (rather than by displaying a colourful plumage or singing like birds). Consequently, there are usually more signs of their presence in relatively accessible places. Most British mammals are small, nocturnal or both and therefore tend to escape notice unless we find them dead (e.g. regurgitated in owl pellets or in discarded bottles) or we use special techniques to catch them (in live traps) or detect them (e.g. hair tubes). Road casualties are also an important source of records of mammals that would often remain undetected. Certain methods are more appropriate for some species than for others. Use Table 4 as a 'prompt list' of signs commonly left by each species.

Some signs can be taken as a direct identification of the species, for example, the spraint of an otter is almost definitive, whereas the dropping of a fallow deer can be confused with other species of deer, or perhaps sheep, except by the experienced eye.

Some signs provide clues which need to be followed up by further investigation to provide a reliable record of the species. A burrow, for example, along with a distinctive footprint beside it, may confirm what species is using the burrow. As soon as you find one sign, look for others in the immediate vicinity to back up the record.

Arrival at the site

First scan the site, a field for example, for obvious signs such as molehills and rabbit burrows. Look on the ground for droppings and tracks, but also up in the trees for signs of squirrels and under bushes for discarded bottles or odd bones. Try to think like a wary mammal. Hedgerows can act as corridors linking patches of denser habitat, such as woodland, with signs scattered along the way. Cross open spaces to inspect features like a gate post for territorial markings such as droppings. (Use Table 4 as a prompt.)

Table 4 Techniques for recording terrestrial British mammals*

❏ Denotes a sign that may be distinctive enough to allow identification to species level by non-specialists. A ring indicates a group of species whose signs are easy to identify as belonging to the group but hard to identify to a particular species.

	Signs						Dead mammals				Traps			
	Burrows	Nests	Footprints/trails	Fur	Droppings/latrines	Feeding signs	Road casualties	Discarded bottles	Owl pellets	Cat kills	Longworths	Nest boxes/tubes	Corrugated iron	Hair tubes
Hedgehog		❏			❏		❏				❏			
Mole	❏						❏		❏	❏				
Common shrew								❏	❏	❏	❏		❏	❏
Pygmy shrew								❏	❏	❏	❏		❏	❏
Water shrew					❏			❏	❏	❏	❏		❏	❏
Rabbit	❏		❏		❏		❏		❏	❏				
Brown hare			❏		❏		❏							
Mountain hare			❏	❏	❏		❏							
Red squirrel		❏				❏	❏			❏	❏			
Grey squirrel		❏				❏	❏			❏	❏			
Bank vole			❏			❏		❏	❏	❏	❏		❏	❏
Field vole			❏			❏		❏	❏	❏	❏		❏	❏
Water vole	❏		❏		❏	❏			❏	❏				
Wood mouse								❏	❏	❏	❏	❏	❏	❏
Yellow-necked mouse								❏	❏	❏	❏	❏	❏	❏
Harvest mouse		❏						❏	❏	❏	❏			❏
House mouse								❏	❏	❏	❏			❏
Brown rat			❏		❏		❏	❏	❏	❏			❏	❏
Hazel dormouse		❏				❏		❏	❏	❏		❏		❏
Edible dormouse							❏		❏		❏			
Fox	❏		❏	❏	❏		❏							
Pine marten					❏		❏							❏
Stoat							❏							
Weasel							❏						❏	
Polecat							❏							
Mink			❏		❏		❏							
Badger	❏		❏	❏	❏	❏	❏							
Otter			❏		❏		❏							
Wildcat							❏							
Red deer			❏		❏	❏	❏							
Sika deer			❏		❏	❏	❏							
Fallow deer			❏		❏	❏	❏							
Roe deer			❏		❏	❏	❏							
Muntjac					❏	❏	❏							
Chinese water deer					❏		❏							
Wild boar			❏			❏	❏							

* Other than sightings of live animals.

Tracks, trails and tracking tunnels

Tracks or footprints are the imprint of the underside of a paw made in damp, soft substrates such as sand or mud. Both tracks and trails are often a good clue but are not generally regarded as reliable records on their own, and usually need following up to obtain a confirmed record.

Tracks

In order for clear tracks to be made that can be identified with confidence a number of conditions need to be satisfied. The substrate needs to have the right consistency and the animal must have left a clean track which has not been smudged or superimposed. It then takes an experienced eye to distinguish species which leave similar tracks, such as a dog from a fox print. Domestic mammal tracks account for around 90% of tracks that one encounters in the countryside, and it is important to be able to recognise these first to allow you to pick out those of wild mammals. Consider the habitat you are in when identifying tracks but keep an open mind at the same time. The pattern of tracks can also be distinctive.

The best conditions for looking for tracks occur when there is fresh snow. Admittedly, this makes your survey planning difficult, but is an opportunity worth pursuing when you can! Tracks made only a few hours earlier are easiest to identify and may tell you something about the animal's behaviour. If it was hunting, the tracks of the predator may lead to the tracks of the prey or if it was courting you may find the tracks of another individual. Bear in mind that in certain circumstances (e.g. in melting snow) the tracks will become enlarged. Tracks of cats, for example, may appear to be more like those of a puma! Tracks can also be clear in shallow mud after rain.

Plaster casts

In firmer, deeper mud a plaster cast of tracks can be taken, especially to detect under-recorded species or species that are locally or nationally rare. Casts allow the track to be examined in three dimensions to confirm identity and can be particularly valuable as proof of presence.

1. Mix water and plaster of Paris (available from chemists) in equal parts. Add plaster to water, stirring to mix well and tap the container to ensure there are no air bubbles.

2. Enclose the track with a mould such as a plastic ring, which can be made by cutting up a plastic container such as a drink bottle or an ice-cream container. Alternatively, make a ring of card held in place by paper clips. Pour in the plaster.

3. Allow the plaster to dry for about 30 minutes (longer in damp weather).

4. Lift the cast, allow it to dry completely, then clean off any mud with a soft brush such as an old tooth brush, or wash it.

5. To create an imprint of the cast, grease it with a layer of petroleum jelly. Surround with a strip of card to contain the wet plaster, and repeat the above procedure.

Identifying mammal tracks

In order to learn particular mammal tracks, it helps to be familiar with the structure of the mammalian foot and how it varies between species. Table 4 indicates species that can be easily identified by their tracks.

The structure of the foot reflects the lifestyle of the animal; fast runners such as deer run on their toes (hooves) whereas those that tend to plod, such as badgers, do so on the whole foot (the paw). Swimmers, such as otters, have webbed feet. Hooved animal tracks display a single large toe (e.g. a horse) or two slots (or cleaves) such as deer and sheep. Dew claws, which are positioned higher up the foot, may show up in deep snow. Non-hooved mammals leave an imprint showing four or five toes around a pad, the sole of the foot, and often claw marks.

Tracks

Insectivores and rodents

There is much overlap in the size and appearance of the tracks of these groups of species. They can rarely be used for positive identification, but you may be able to assign them to their respective groups. The hind feet of both insectivores and rodents have five toes and claws, insectivores (hedgehog, mole and shrews) show five toes on their fore foot, whereas rodents show only four. These tiny tracks are unlikely to be visible except in very fine mud or as prints on a tracking board or in a tracking tunnel.

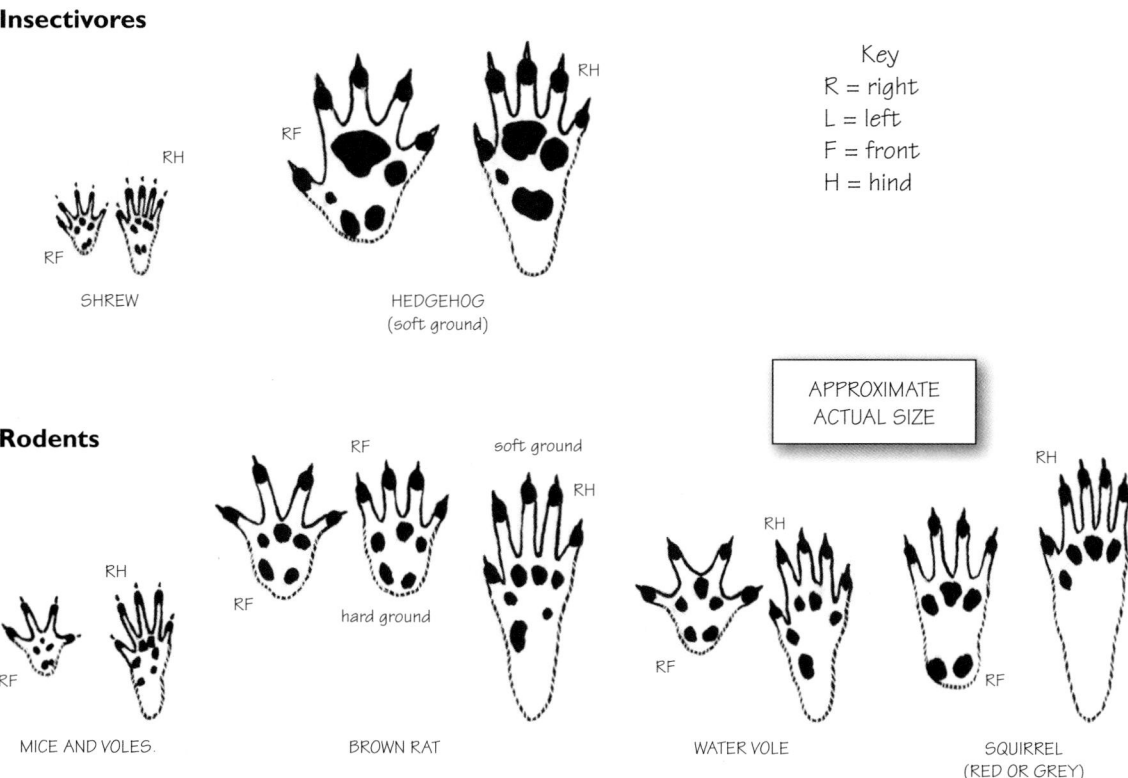

Rabbits and hares

The position of the feet is the most distinctive feature of rabbit and hare tracks, with the long hind feet parallel and the forefootprints often between them, depending on speed of travel.

Carnivores

Fox, dog and cat

Foxes and cats leave a similar pattern of tracks in a straight line with one foot placed directly in front of another. The prints can be distinguished by the absence of claws in cats. Dog prints vary in size according to the breed but the shape is consistently different from foxes. Dog prints are as broad as they are long whereas fox prints are longer and narrower; diamond-shaped. The plantar pad ('palm') on the fox's hind foot, is only a little larger than the toe prints. In dogs it is much larger. The tracks of a fox usually shows a purposeful path, with footprints directly ahead of each other. In trails made by dogs the footprints are staggered alternately to the right and left of the line of travel.

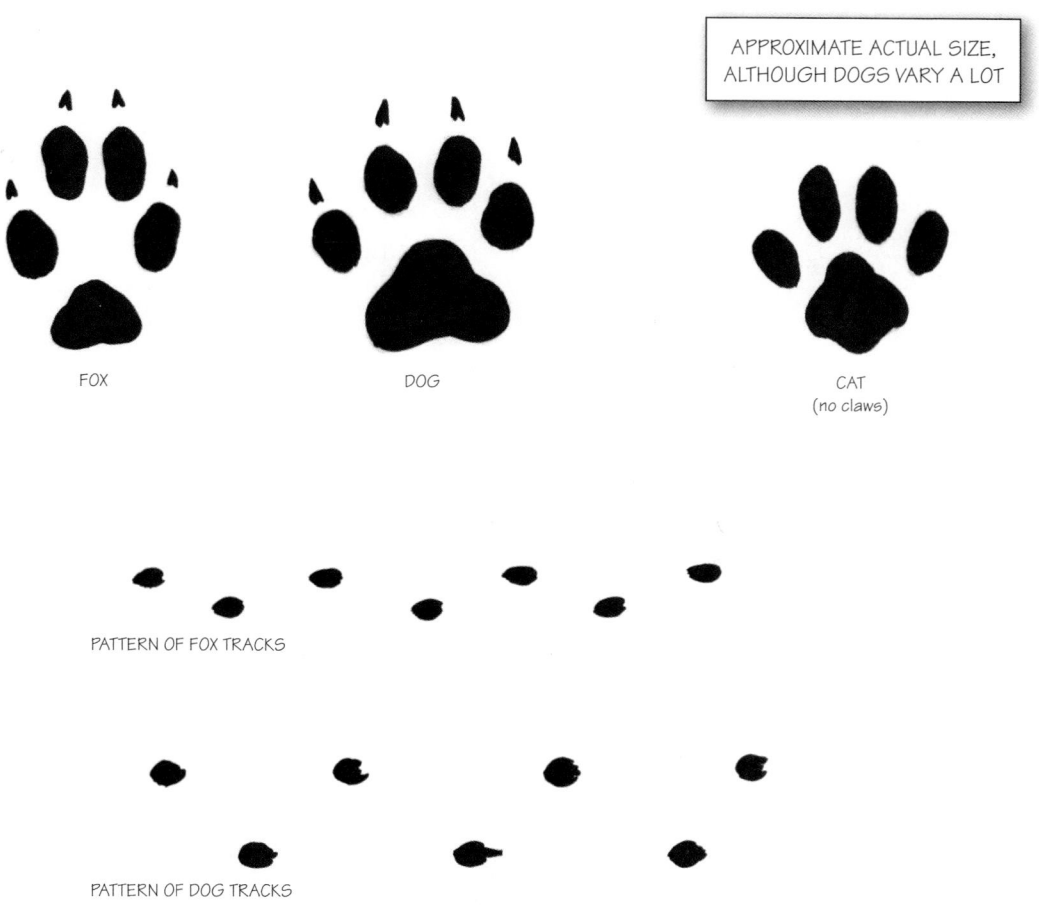

Mustelids

Mustelids tend to use a lolloping gait, due to their long body, except weasels which appear to run more evenly and badgers which amble. All leave a trail showing groups of three or four footprints. All have a print showing five toes around a central pad although sometimes only four register.

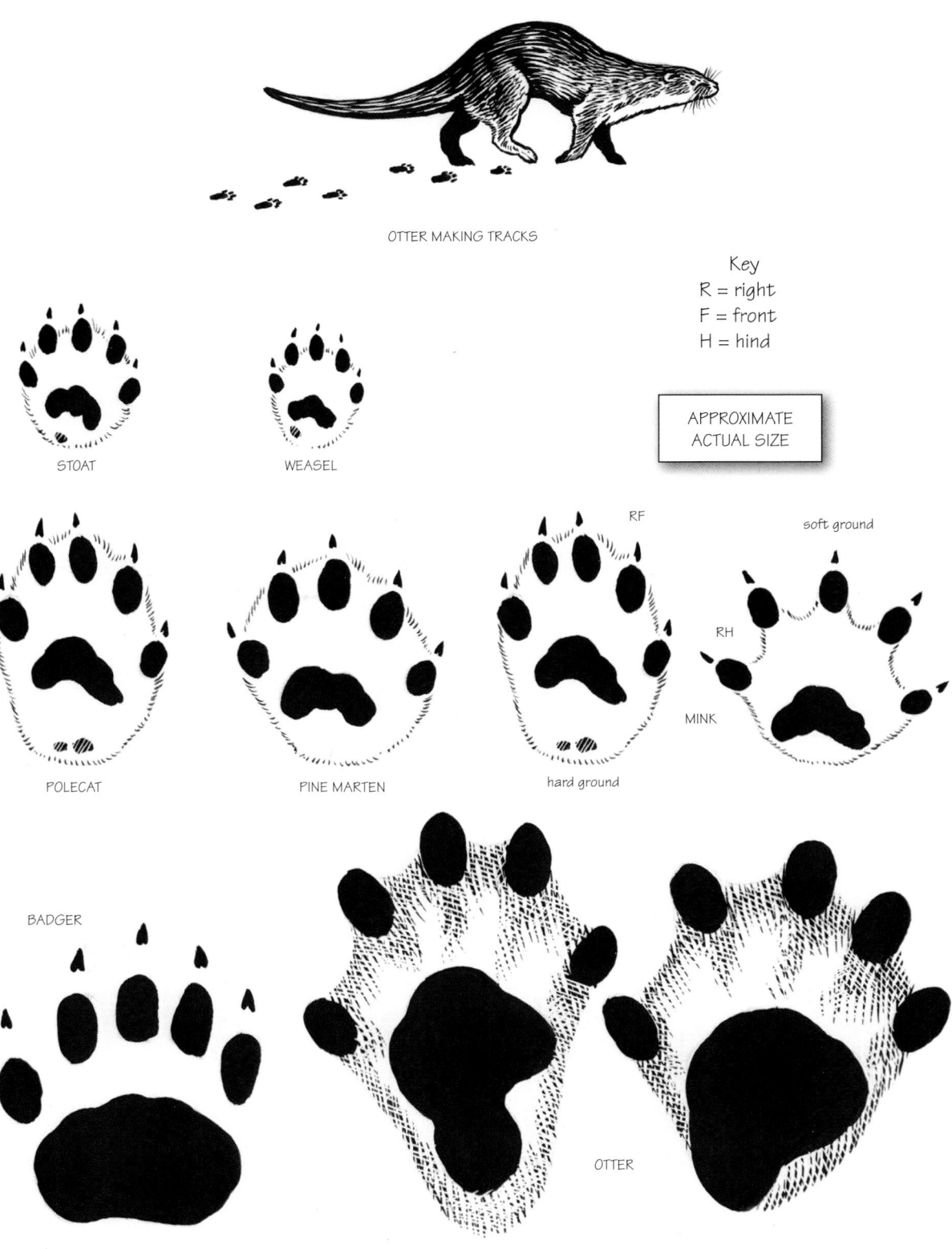

Ungulates

Deer, sheep, goats and wild boar

Deer prints vary in size with species but are fairly similar in shape. The shape, however, can vary according to how fast the animal is moving. When walking, deer tracks show two parallel bars but these become more splayed the faster the animal moves.

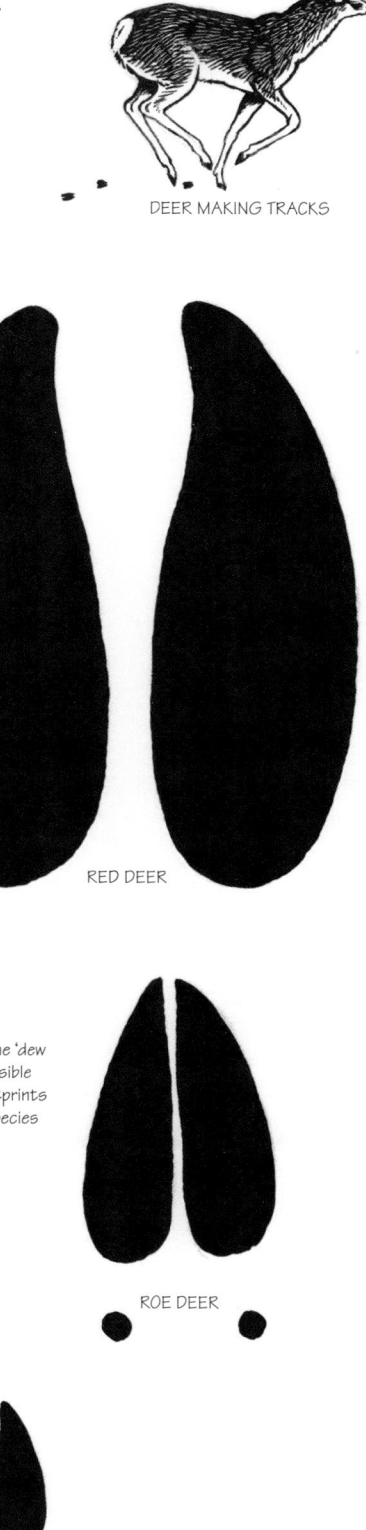

DEER MAKING TRACKS

SIKA DEER

RED DEER

APPROXIMATE ACTUAL SIZE

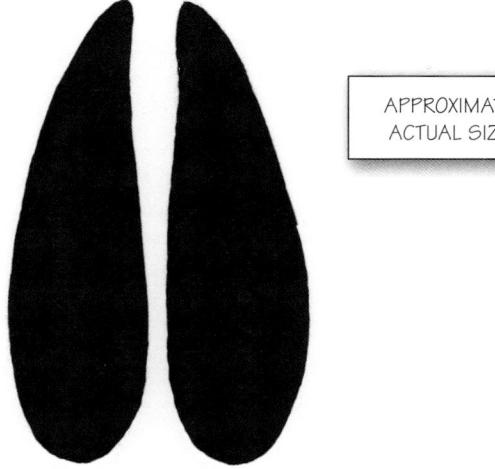

FALLOW DEER

Marks made by the 'dew claws' may be visible sometimes in footprints of the smaller species

ROE DEER

CHINESE WATER DEER

MUNTJAC

How to Find and Identify Mammals
The Mammal Society

APPROXIMATE ACTUAL SIZE

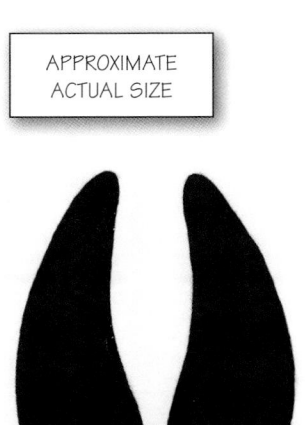
SHEEP

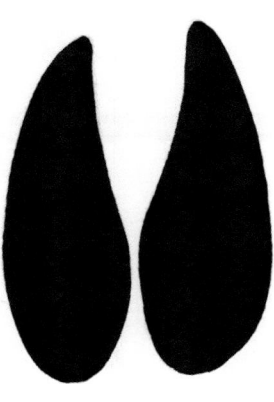
GOAT

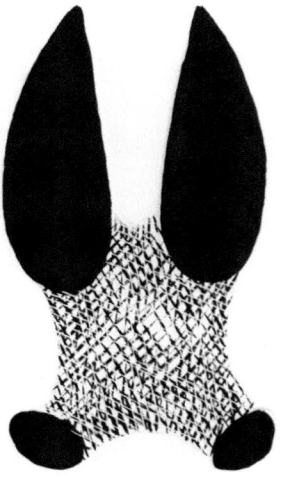
WILD BOAR

Trails

Trails form where the passage of an animal has caused disturbance to the substrate and vegetation. Badgers tend to form the most prominent trails which often lead from their setts to feeding grounds. Persistent use erodes and compacts the soil and slows the growth of grass on the trail, although vegetation may close over the top, forming a tunnel. Temporary trails can also be formed in early morning dew by passing mammals.

Investigate any linear features such as worn-looking paths. Paths may lead under fences and reveal further signs such as droppings, or fur caught on barbed wire or brambles. If the path leads to damp ground, perhaps by a river, stream or pond, it may be possible to determine tracks in the mud. Trails may also lead you to the animal's burrow or nest site and enable you to identify the species.

Tracker boards consist of a tile covered in soot created by holding the tile over a candle. They can be used to detect the passage of small mammals, including small mustelids.

FOOTPRINT OR TRACKER TUNNELS (IN WHICH MAMMALS LEAVE INKY FOOTPRINTS ON A SHEET OF PAPER) ARE AVAILABLE FROM THE MAMMAL SOCIETY (SEE p.44 FOR DETAILS ON HOW TO USE IT).

Droppings and latrines

Some mammals identify and communicate with each other by scent and leave their droppings in particular locations. These may have a distinctive scent. Other mammals do not use their droppings for communication and deposit them at random.

The droppings of insectivores are usually sausage-shaped, and have a tendency to crumble into fragments of insect remains. Herbivores (including squirrels) eat large quantities of vegetation and leave clusters of 10–20 pellets. These tend to be spherical or pellet-shaped and have a uniform texture. Carnivores (and hedgehogs) tend to produce single, sausage-shaped droppings that normally contain fur, bone or insect fragments. Bones are normally shattered, whereas in owl pellets the bones and the skulls of the prey are usually mostly intact.

All British carnivores are mustelids, except for the fox and the wildcat. Musk glands at the base of the tail are particularly well developed in mustelids, and fresh droppings, which usually have hair and fur inside, and sometimes fragmented bones, smell of musk. These can be distinguished from owl pellets, which contain intact bones and skulls.

Variations in an animal's diet, digestion and 'extrusion dynamics' lead to distinct variations in content, colour, texture, smell, size and shape of droppings.

Small mammal droppings (shorter than 1cm) are very difficult to identify to species and are therefore not described in detail. An exception to this are the droppings of water shrews which are less than 0.5cm in length and are the only small mammal droppings containing fragments of aquatic insects and crustaceans, but recognising these is a specialist task (see Appendix 6).

Droppings – shorter than 1cm

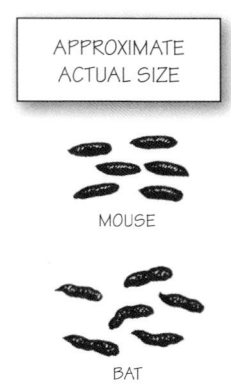

APPROXIMATE ACTUAL SIZE

MOUSE

BAT

Features	Mouse	Bat
Smell	House mouse – strong urine. Other mice – not so strong or no smell	Usually little or no smell
Texture	Very hard when dry – doesn't crumble	When dry crumbles to dust (insect remains)
Usual location	Small heaps almost anywhere	Large heaps under roosts, or singly below feeding places or stuck to walls and doors

Herbivore droppings – about 1cm or longer

Colours vary a lot depending on what has been eaten. Squirrels feeding on pollen for example will produce yellowish droppings.

Features	Water vole	Rat	Squirrel
Smell	Odourless	Foul, rancid	Depends upon diet but often sweet, hint of pine sawdust
Colour	Variable – usually dark green when broken up	Blackish brown	Dark grey/black
Usual location	Latrines and small heaps close to water	In or near buildings	Near trees

WATER VOLE

RAT

SQUIRREL

Herbivore droppings – spherical or more than 1cm long

Appearance varies according to season, moisture content and freshness.
Rabbit and hare make spherical pellets, other herbivores have oval droppings.

Features	Rabbit	Hare
Smell	Sweet, damp digestive biscuit/hint of mown hay	Sweet, damp digestive biscuit/hint of mown hay
Colour	Yellowish brown-green	Greenish-brown
Distinctive features	May be found in dense aggregations of pellets on prominent feature, e.g. anthill	Larger and more flattened than rabbit, however, variable and dependent on diet

RABBIT

HARE

Deer

Features	Red	Fallow	Sika
No obvious smell or colour variation			

Features	Roe	Muntjac	Chinese water deer	Sheep
No obvious smell or colour variation				

Insectivores

Features	Hedgehog
Smell	Sweet, hint of linseed oil
Colour	Blue-black
Distinctive features	Crinkly, often studded with shiny fragments of insect cuticle

APPROXIMATE ACTUAL SIZE

Carnivores

Droppings are usually deposited singly and often contain hair or bits of bone.

Features	Pine marten	Stoat	Weasel
Smell	Sweet, violets when fresh	Musky, but not too unpleasant	Musky
Colour	Blackish	Blackish brown	Brown

Features	Polecat	Mink
Smell	Foul, foetid meat, distinctly unpleasant	Foul, burnt rubber, rotten meat, unpleasant
Colour	Blackish	Greenish, black, brown
Distinctive features	Deposited in prominent places	More bones than polecat but often found at similar sites and along river banks

Features	Badger	Otter
Smell	Foul, strong musk, oily, hint of hay	Sweet, jasmine tea, laurel flowers, slightly oily rag, distinctive. Can have a tarry smell. Often in very small quantities
Colour	Blue-black-brown	Greenish, black-grey
Distinctive features	Often containing seeds and large bits inside. A purple colour may be due to eating blackberries. A formless mud-like dung is very common when large numbers of earthworms have been eaten	Contains mainly fish scales, bones, shells of crustaceans, feathers or fur
Usual location	Often located in a small pit or 'latrine'	Smeared on to rocks or logs close to water

APPROXIMATE ACTUAL SIZE

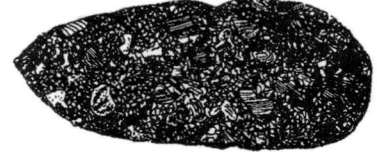

Fox

Fox droppings usually have a twisted appearance, with a tapering 'tail' at one end. They are normally greyish, full of fur, bone fragments and often fruit pips. Droppings of domestic cats and dogs are a similar size (about 5cm long), but are not twisted and the texture is uniform, usually without bits of fur, bone or plant.

BADGER LATRINE – DROPPINGS ARE SLOPPY AND SHAPELESS

OTTER SPRAINT MARK – DROPPINGS ARE OFTEN SMEARED ON TO A STONE OR LOG

Feeding signs

Nibbled stalks of grass

Nibbled stalks of grass in small piles among tunnels in long grass indicate the presence of field voles. Where these are found along a river bank or canal they may indicate the presence of water voles and may incorporate a latrine (see Droppings and latrines for illustration).

FIELD VOLE FEEDING REMAINS

Gnawed or shattered hazel nuts

These are likely to be the food remains of bank vole, wood mouse, hazel dormouse, squirrel or bird. The species can be identified by the gnawed marks on the nut. Squirrels and birds split the nut leaving jagged edges and irregular pieces whereas the other three species gnaw a hole in a characteristic pattern.

Hazel dormouse

Scratchy gnaw marks on outer edge of hole with smooth, scooped out inner ring. Hole is almost circular with toothmarks running along the cut edge.

Squirrel

Prised apart through a hole in top of nut. Leaves jagged fragments or half nutshells.

Wood mouse

Toothmarks on outside surface of nut. Toothmarks go across the cut edge of the hole.

Bank vole

No marks on shell surface. Gnawed toothmarks go across the cut edge of the hole.

Burrows

Burrows are sometimes easiest to locate during the breeding season when activity is high and foraging parents produce well-worn thoroughfares. The young may emerge but are unlikely to stray far. At other times of year, when the vegetation is low, it may be easier to spot burrows although there may be less activity.

Burrows of large mammals are generally located beside some kind of shelter such as a hedge or bank that gives the emerging animals protection. Outside the breeding season some mammals change burrow sites quite regularly. Wood mice, stoats, weasels and foxes sometimes appropriate a nest or burrow built by another species.

The table below indicates approximate relative sizes of burrows of different species; it is meant as a guide, as sometimes individuals may have particularly large burrows that fall outside the range indicated, especially in soft sandy soils.

Size	Diameter	How to remember size	Likely species
Small	Less than 4cm	Ping pong ball-sized, 50p coin	Small mammals, i.e. mice and voles
Small to medium	4–8cm	Tennis ball-size	Mole, water vole, rat
Medium to large	8–20cm	Fist-sized or larger	Rabbit
Large	More than 20cm	Football-sized	Fox or badger

Identification of burrows

Small burrows – less than 4cm diameter

If food (seeds and berries) has been collected near the entrance of a small burrow, it probably belongs to a wood mouse or bank vole (F. Tattersall pers. comm.). House mice, which are generally restricted to buildings, can form distinctive holes in the wall and floor, creating greasy smears around the entrance. They often leave lots of gnawed food remains near the entrance and may leave a characteristic strong musty (acetamide) smell of urine. Live traps set at the burrow entrance can be used to catch and identify mammals in occupation. Alternatively a tracker board or tunnel can be used. You could also try positioning sticky tape above the burrow, though not obstructing it, to collect hairs from animals passing in and out. These can be identified using a lens or microscope.

In dense grass, field voles often create a maze of runways just above ground level. Often these are exposed when snow melts. Burrows frequently occur under corrugated iron sheeting left lying flat on the ground (see Corrugated iron sheets).

Small to medium-sized burrows – 4 to 8cm diameter

Mole

The characteristic spoil heaps of molehills are familiar to most people. Molehills consist of pure loose soil. Anthills are usually firmer, consolidated by vegetation and roots – and usually have ants in them! Anthills also often have rabbit droppings on top.

Water vole and brown rat

Water voles and brown rats create burrows of similar size, within about 1m of river banks. Breeding water voles may have a 'lawn' of nibbled grass in front of the entrance due to their habit of grazing in close proximity to their burrow. Brown rats, however, tend to have a fan of excavated soil in front of the entrance holes and are joined by well-worn 'rat runs' which may even pass under water. In the breeding season water voles also have several 'latrines' within their territory, which have a pile of dark green droppings, some of which may have been trodden into a mush. Rats generally make their burrows near a food source and may also leave droppings nearby.

WATER VOLE BURROWS

RAT BURROWS LINKED BY 'RAT RUNS'

Medium-sized burrows – 8 to 20cm diameter
Rabbit

Rabbit burrows are especially prevalent on well-drained slopes. The entrance diameter can vary, but is generally about 10cm. Rabbit burrows characteristically occur in clusters in close proximity to each other. Hares do not make burrows.

Large burrows – more than 20cm diameter
Fox and badger

Badger setts account for nearly 60% of records of badgers. They are particularly abundant on slopes on sandy soils. Setts consist of multiple holes, sometimes 50 or more. Fox 'earths' (which account for less than 2% of fox records) usually have only one entrance and tend to develop a 'foxy' smell. When the cubs are emerging the surrounding vegetation may be flattened, and feathers, chewed bits of wood and bones may be strewn about the entrance. In contrast, badgers do not usually leave food debris lying about, although there is often a large heap of earth, bedding and dry grass thrown out in front of the entrance to the sett. This often contains badger hair which is distinctive. These hairs are long, wiry and white with a broad black zone towards one end and tend to be slightly wavy, not dead straight (see Mammal identification from hairs). Tracks in soil surrounding the entrance may also indicate the species of the user.

Badger setts tend to have more than two entrances. Foxes, which are not equipped with such powerful digging apparatus as badgers, dig smaller and shallower burrows, tend not to create more than two openings and have a smaller spoil heap at the entrance. To confuse the matter, foxes often take over old badger setts.

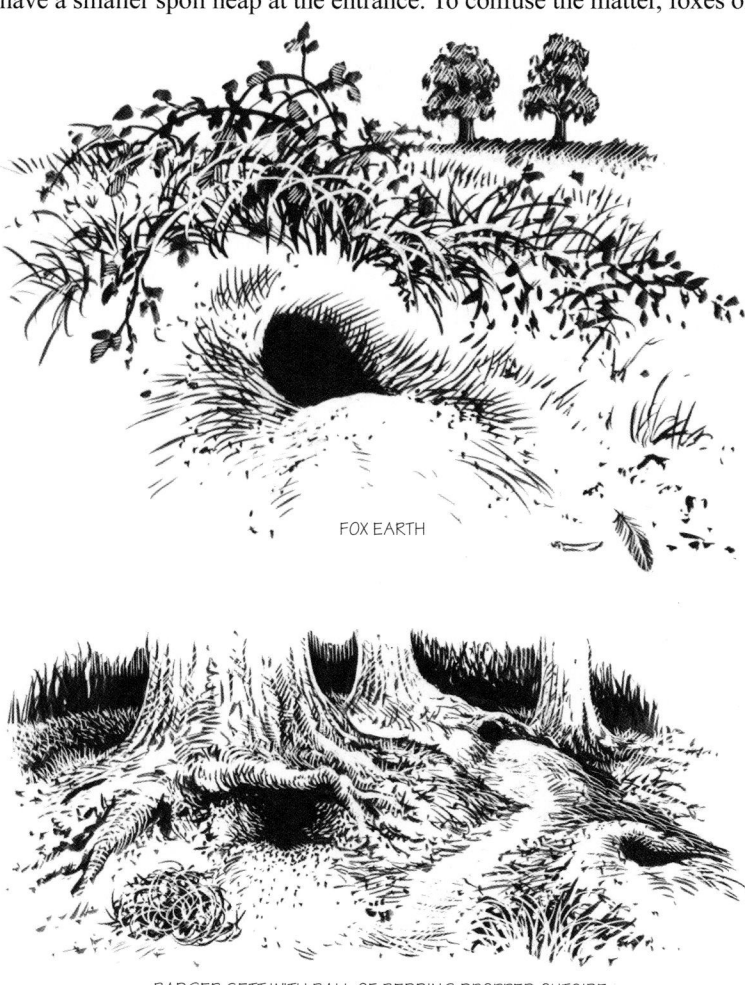

FOX EARTH

BADGER SETT WITH BALL OF BEDDING DROPPED OUTSIDE.
Badger setts also often have distinct well-trodden paths leading from entrance holes.

Otter and mink

Both species live close to the water's edge. Otters make holts in cavities under roots of bankside trees or boulders, but may also rest in couches of flattened vegetation or scraped out soil, often concealed by surrounding vegetation. Mink will also make dens in the hollows of bankside trees.

OTTER HOLT

OTTER COUCH

Other types of hole

Dormice, squirrels and pine martens make use of holes in trees. However, a hole in a tree cannot be taken as a reliable record. If you find a hole you believe is used by one of these species, try to find other signs to back up the record.

Nests

Mammals which build nests above ground include hedgehogs, harvest mice, dormice and squirrels.

Red and grey squirrel

The nests of red and grey squirrels are known as 'dreys'. They are spherical collections of twigs and leaves which are generally (but not always) located in a fork in the branches close to the trunk, usually from 6m up. They are most easily seen in winter when there are no leaves on the trees. It is not generally possible to distinguish between the dreys of red and grey squirrels. The nests of similar size built by magpies, crows and other birds can be recognised by the fact that they are made with dead twigs and tend not to incorporate leaves. They are usually located further from the tree trunk.

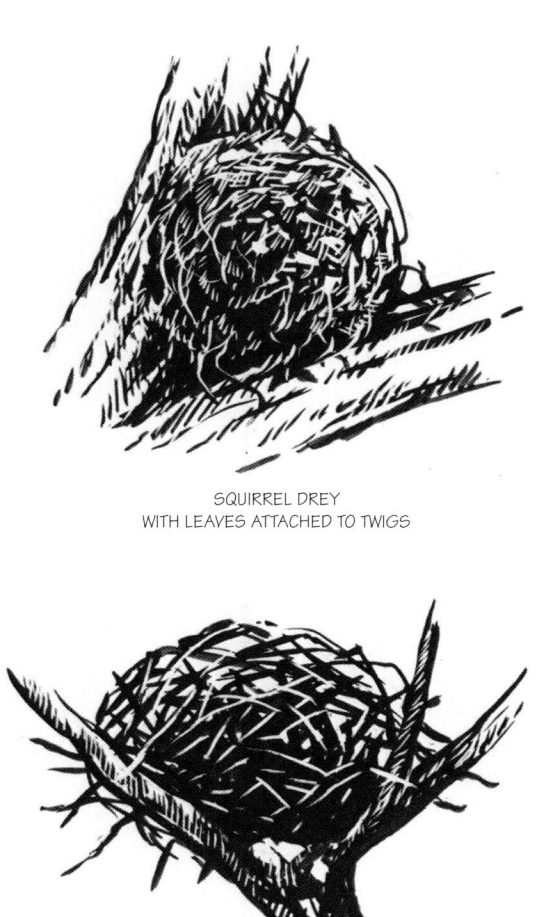

SQUIRREL DREY
WITH LEAVES ATTACHED TO TWIGS

CROW OR MAGPIE NEST
MADE OF DEAD TWIGS SO NO ATTACHED LEAVES

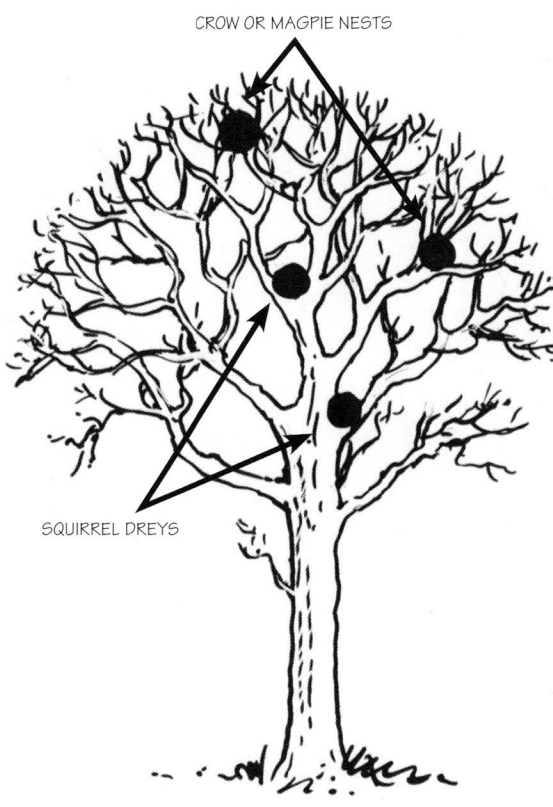

POSITION OF SQUIRREL AND CROW OR MAGPIE NESTS IN TREE, ALTHOUGH SQUIRREL SUMMER DREYS CAN BE POSITIONED FURTHER AWAY FROM THE MAIN TRUNK

Identification of some distinctive small mammal nests

	Harvest mouse	**Hazel dormouse**	**Hedgehog**
When to find nests	Easiest in early autumn	Summer/winter	Easiest in late winter
Where to look for nests	Farmland, hedgerows, patches of tall stiff-stemmed grasses and reeds	Coppiced hazel woodlands especially in bramble	In sheltered cavities, e.g. between logs in hedgerows, gardens, farmland and under low brambles
Height above ground	Depends on height of the supporting plants (see diagram overleaf). Up to 1.5m	1–2m off the ground especially in bramble. Tightly woven hibernation nests may be found on the ground, underneath leaves, moss, logs or tree stumps	On the ground
Size of nest	Golfball to cricket ball-sized	Grapefruit-sized	50cm diameter, slightly flattened
Distinguishing features of nest	Harvest mouse nests are domed, not cup-shaped like bird nests. Composed of leaves of grasses shredded longitudinally, some of which are still attached to the stems. The nest, therefore, appears to hang from the surrounding stems. Nests of reed warblers have stems of supporting plants passing through the nest, not incorporated into the nest material itself	May contain woody species woven into the nest, such as strips of honeysuckle bark with an outer layer of leaves. No distinct entrance hole, like a wren's nest, and no feathers inside	Composed of leaves, grass and other materials. The leaves are gathered into a heap and the hedgehog then shuffles around inside until the leaves become similarly orientated and packed flat against each other

Harvest mouse

The harvest mouse is an under-recorded species. In summer, harvest mice spend most of their active hours climbing in long grasses and tend not to be caught in Longworth traps, which are usually set on the ground. The incidence of harvest mice in owl pellets is low compared with other small mammals. The characteristic breeding nests, however, provide obvious signs of the presence of harvest mice and are unlikely to be confused with other types of nest. Looking for nests requires less effort than trapping the animals themselves and allows a large number of sites to be surveyed in one day. Look in long grass, reedbeds, tall 'weeds' and hedgerows. Nests are not usually found in cornfields, except possibly at the edges. Do not trample crops!

HARVEST MOUSE AND ITS NEST

POSITION OF HARVEST MOUSE NESTS IN DIFFERENT VEGETATION TYPES:

IN REEDS (e.g. Phalaris),
LONG GRASSES AND CEREALS

IN PLANTS THAT FORM TUSSOCKS OF LEAVES
AT THE BASE OF THE FLOWERING STEMS,
e.g. cocksfoot (Dactylis glomerata),
tuffed hair grass (Deschampsia caespitosa and Molinia spp.)

Hazel dormouse

Dormice spend most of their time in trees and overgrown hedgerows and are rarely caught in Longworth traps. Apart from using their own nests, dormice may use a deserted bird nest or a nest box.

HAZEL DORMOUSE SUMMER NEST

Summer nests are usually made of shredded plant material woven into a ball about the size of a grapefruit. They may incorporate loose tree leaves (not grass leaves attached to their stems as in harvest mouse nests). There is usually no distinct entrance hole like in a wren's nest. They are easiest to find in late autumn by gently pulling bramble bushes apart using a garden rake. Hibernation nests are more difficult to locate. They are built on the ground, usually under moss or leaves. They are tightly woven, tennis ball-sized, and made of shredded fibrous material (e.g. honeysuckle bark).

Edible dormouse

The edible dormouse often uses deserted squirrel dreys, tree holes, cavities in roof spaces or large bird nest boxes in summer. In winter they hibernate underground without nesting material and are unlikely to be found.

Hedgehog hibernation nests

Hedgehogs may build several nests in the course of one winter. These tend to be tucked under a bush, log pile, garden shed or anywhere that offers support and protection. They consist of a tightly-packed mass of dead leaves.

HEDGEHOG WINTER NEST

Corrugated iron sheets (and other debris such as pieces of hardboard and plywood)

Small mammals are often attracted to the warm, sheltered conditions generated underneath a sheet of metal or other building material. The sheet can be lifted quickly to catch animals sheltering beneath it. This method can be used to improve the chance of recording voles, mice and shrews.

Sheets of metal or wood can be inspected several times during the season and it may be worth noting where they are on a map. Do not place these sheets on other people's land without asking permission, but make use of any that are already in place.

Size of sheet

The more sheets you inspect the more likely you will get a positive record. The main influence may be the size of sheet you can carry to the site and turn over quickly when checking. A sheet of around 0.5m x 1.5m is ideal.

How to position the sheet

Get permission from the landowner first. Position the sheet where the sunlight can warm it, but not too much or the sheet will become very hot. Try to locate it near some cover to provide a mixture of sun and partial shade. Try to position the sheet on grass. Before checking for mammals, wait a few weeks until the grass has died back underneath.

How to turn over the sheet – hints on handling

Two people should be present, one to lift the sheet and one, wearing gloves, to swiftly grab any small mammals underneath. The 'catcher' may find it easier to gently pin the animal down with the palm of one hand and then to get the scruff of the neck with the other hand. Alternatively, place a piece of cloth over the animal before gripping it. Small mammals should not be held by the tail.

 Be aware that adders and other reptiles also favour the conditions found under metal sheets in sunny positions.

Field Note 3: Recording small mammals under corrugated iron

> I saw and caught my first yellow-necked mouse under a sheet of corrugated iron (and at least nine other species at different times)!
>
> *Pat Morris*

Bait stations for water shrews and dormice

Water shrews will readily investigate novel objects, particularly if a food source is detected. Bait stations are composed of a length of plastic piping (20cm long; 4cm diameter) with muslin netting held over one end by an elastic band. By providing a suitable food source (e.g. blowfly pupae), these tubes encourage visiting shrews (and other small mammals) to enter, feed and defecate. The droppings of water shrews can be distinguished from other small mammals by the presence of the remains of distinctive bits of aquatic prey. For illustrations of the characteristic remains of aquatic insects in water shrew droppings see Appendix 6.

Empty opened milk cartons, baited with apple and wedged in bushes, have been used to detect dormice. Their droppings left at bait stations are thicker than those of mice and appear crinkled. However, a reference collection of mouse droppings is needed for comparison. This is not a fully reliable technique.

Hedgehog footprint tunnels

Footprint or tracker tunnels, available from The Mammal Society, are placed in suitable edge habitat overnight. Baited with hot dogs and set with ink pads, hedgehogs and other small mammals, leave behind footprints as they safely pass through.

Mammal identification from hairs

The coat of most mammals is composed of a layer of fluffy insulating hair, 'underfur', with a thin layer of stiffer, longer guard hairs on the outside and particularly on the back of the animal. The guard hairs are the easiest to identify visually and are often caught as the animal passes and presses against something sharp such as barbed-wire fencing or brambles, or something sticky. Identification by eye, however, is not always easy (except for badger hairs) and it can sometimes be hard to match what you can see through the microscope with the pictures in a book. Only intact hairs should be used for identification. Do not use parts that have been damaged by a sticky surface.

BADGER HAIR : ACTUAL SIZE
NB crinkly, with black band and white pointed tip

FUR CAUGHT ON BARBED WIRE
Other mammals have shorter fur and the hairs are straight and usually brown.

Guard hairs can be identified according to their colour, length, form and structure. The scales on the outer surface of the hairs are also distinctive but are hard to see under a light microscope without special preparation.

Preparation for examining small hairs under a microscope

1. Dissolve a few grains of gelatin in half a small egg cup of water, paint a thin layer on to a microscope slide and leave to set for 10 minutes. Alternatively try using a nail-varnish film on a microscope slide instead of gelatine, letting it dry until tacky.
2. Select a few stiff guard hairs. Do not use fine or crinkly ones.
3. Place a few hairs on the gelatine film and leave for 30 minutes to set.
4. Peel off the hairs using tweezers and examine the impression of the hair surface scales under the microscope at x50–100 magnification. The most characteristic part of the hair for identification purposes is the 'shield' (the mid to upper third of the hair).
5. Hairs may also be viewed directly under the microscope to see the structure of the medulla (core). (See Teerink, B.J. (2004) *Hair of West European Mammals: Atlas and Identification Key*.)

Hair tubes

Hair tubes are lengths of tubing (generally stiff plastic) about 10cm long that are positioned in sites where they are likely to be used as a tunnel by mammals of an appropriate size. The 'roof' inside the tube is lined with sticky tape, such as carpet tape, to trap hairs from passing mammals and which can be removed for identification. The diameter of the tube should be determined by the type and size of mammal you are attempting to record, although it is possible to raise the level of the 'floor' by pouring in and setting plaster of Paris, or glueing in a rigid strip of waterproof material. Seeds in a matrix of peanut butter is an attractive bait to use for small mammals and can be smeared on the inside of the tube. Tubes need to be fixed in place using sticky tape.

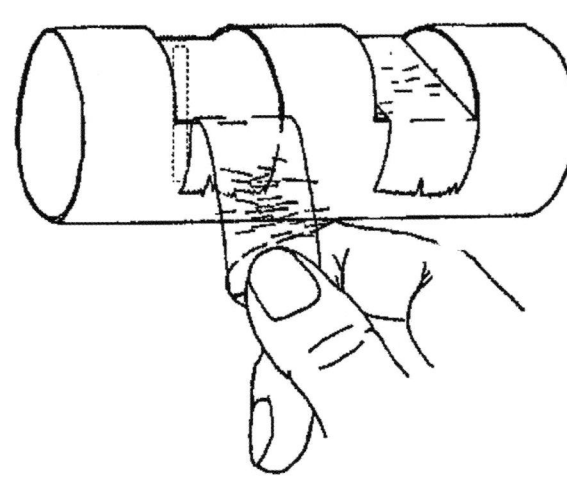

HAIR TUBE WITH STICKY TAPE AND ADHERING HAIRS

Hair tube diameters

Species	Hair tube diameter (cm)
Common shrew	3.0
Pygmy shrew	2.5
Water shrew	3.5
Bank vole	3.5–4.0
Field vole	3.5–4.0
Wood mouse	3.5

Species	Hair tube diameter (cm)
Yellow-necked mouse	4.0
Harvest mouse	3.0
House mouse	3.5
Hazel dormouse	3.5
Squirrel	6–8

DNA-based mammal identification (faeces or hairs)

There has been increasing interest in the use of DNA for mammal identification. This is particularly useful with non-invasively collected samples such as droppings, hairs and feeding remains. Faecal DNA analysis can be used to identify mammals even from very small samples such as harvest mouse or pygmy shrew faeces. DNA analysis depends on the presence of gut epithelial cells in the faecal sample. Animal cells contain DNA in the nucleus and in the mitochondria and as the cell contains between 200 and 10,000 mitochondria, depending on cell type, the mitochondria are a better source of DNA for species identification than the nuclear DNA. This technique can be used to identify the mammal that has deposited the scat/pellet or, with carnivores and predatory birds, it can be used to identify their prey by targeting the DNA of specific small mammals. Hairs plucked from the skin (by sticky tape for example) also have sufficient DNA at their base to permit identification. If you want to use this technique, contact The Mammal Society office for advice as it costs money and requires care to avoid contamination of samples.

Part 5 Recording dead mammals and parts of mammals

Road casualties

Equipment:
1. General recording form and, if possible, a dictaphone.
2. Clip recording form on to dashboard or keep in glove compartment with a pencil so you can easily stop and make a note, or your passenger can do this.
3. Ordnance Survey maps or GPS with grid co-ordinate capability.
4. Bin liners for those likely to find polecats or polecat-ferrets (these should then be sent for confirmation to Andrew Kitchener, Dept. of Natural History, Royal Museum of Scotland, Chambers Street, Edinburgh EH1 1JF).
5. Small plastic bags to use as gloves and to collect hair which, in difficult cases, you may need to send to your County Mammal Recorder for identification or confirmation.
6. Sellotape to stick hair to a sheet of paper with details of the record, and envelopes to put it in.

Examining mammals killed on roads allows us to keep records of some larger, more elusive species, and sometimes confirms the presence of rare species. This method probably under-samples small mammals as their carcasses are harder to see from a moving car and are more likely to be carried off whole by scavengers. Table 4 indicates mammals most likely to be recorded killed on roads. This is the main method of gathering records for some species (e.g. hedgehog, pine marten) and a very important one for others (e.g. stoat, otter, wildcat and brown hare).

Early morning is the best time to collect records of road kills, as mammals tend to be knocked down at night when they are likely to be confused by oncoming headlights and when they are also most active. Mammals squashed overnight will be easier to inspect early in the day before further traffic squashes them even more.

It is often possible to reliably identify a large carcass at 40mph. A dictaphone is useful for recording the details although you should stop the car to do this. If you can't identify the carcass, stop for a closer look from the verge. If you need verification collect some hair, attach it to sellotape and send to your County Mammal Recorder, for possible identification.

Field Note 4: Recording mammal road kills

> In the summer of 1993 the body of an otter on a road 20km from London confirmed the return of this species to the River Thames.
>
> *Rob Strachan*

Leaving the car to retrieve carcasses

Safety for yourself and other road users is the paramount consideration. Traffic on busier roads tends to result in more squashed mammals. To prevent becoming one yourself follow these guidelines.

Never collect on motorways as it is illegal to stop on the hard shoulder except in an emergency. Some busy roads often have parking lay-bys at frequent intervals which are worth using. If there are no lay-bys try to return to the site and park about 30m ahead of the carcass using the car as a shield, pulling on to the extreme nearside. Put on your hazard warning lights and, subject to traffic flow, leave the car from the verge side. Wear a 'high visibility' jacket if possible and walk up the verge rather than the kerb. When the road is clear retrieve the carcass quickly by lifting it on to a bin liner and carrying it back to the car.

It may be worth contacting your local motorway services and county council department responsible for retrieving carcasses from roads, and supply them with mammal recording forms to return to the County Mammal Recorder.

Discarded glass bottles

Equipment:
1. Disposable gloves or clear plastic bags.
2. Water, dish (plate or piece of paper) on which to tip contents of bottle for inspection.
3. Small mammal skull identification key.
4. Plastic pot for specimens.
5. Forceps and hand lens.

Over 100,000,000 bottles a year are lost from circulation. Apart from contributing to Britain's litter problem, many of these bottles trap small mammals, depending on where they are positioned (Morris & Harper 1965). Although most bottles that have trapped mammals contain only one or two, a milk bottle found in Essex contained 28 small mammals. About 5% of bottles containing mammals have killed more than seven. Old milk bottles are the ones most likely to have caught mammals (about 10% of the ones you inspect). Beer bottles and fizzy drink bottles have narrower necks and catch mammals less often. Plastic bottles rarely catch mammals. Ring-pull drink cans also kill mammals, usually shrews. Less than 1% of cans inspected are likely to contain victims.

Mammals probably enter out of curiosity or in search of food. Entering may be comparatively easy especially if the bottle neck is pointing up. Escape is harder as the animal must push on slippery glass and against a narrowing neck. Animals perish from cold or starvation. Prevent further deaths by collecting and disposing of bottles or positioning them with the neck stuck into the soil and pointing downhill. Never deliberately put out bottles to catch animals!

As bottles have sometimes been in place for extended periods they sometimes account for records of species which are rare and not commonly found by other methods (e.g. water shrew). Bottles provide a useful starting point when drawing up a species list for a site and are also useful for sampling inaccessible habitats where the repeated visits required by live trapping are inconvenient. Common shrews are the most frequent captures and, along with the wood mouse and bank vole, account for over 90% of all mammals in bottles.

The best season for bottle surveys is late winter when the vegetation is low and bottles are easiest to find. Tip out the contents of the bottle and wash away material other than bones. Pick out the skulls and identify them using the key in Appendix 5.

Field Note 5: **Recording mammals in discarded bottles**

> Bottles are highly effective, lethal mammal traps. By collecting discarded bottles that lie strewn about the countryside, you can save many small mammals from an unpleasant end and gather useful records at the same time. The altitude record for the pygmy shrew, for example, came from a bottle near the peak of Ben Nevis. There can be further bonuses – I once found an unopened bottle of champagne in a ditch! Do not put out bottles specially to catch mammals: there are already millions of them littering the countryside.
>
> *Pat Morris*

Owl pellets

Equipment:
1. Disposable gloves or clear plastic bags.
2. Water, dish (plate or piece of paper) on which to dissect pellets for inspection.
3. Small mammal skull identification key.
4. Plastic pot for specimens.
5. Forceps and hand lens.
6. Owl pellet recording form.

Owls are one of the most effective hunters of small mammals. They swallow their prey whole, digest the flesh and then regurgitate the undigested remains in neat pellets of bones and fur. Analysis of the contents of pellets allows the small mammal community to be studied (with a bias towards mammals which are favoured prey) and can be particularly useful for sampling less common species which are unlikely to be found in the course of small-scale trapping efforts.

Barn owl pellets are the easiest to study as they tend to use sheltered roosts, such as outbuildings, where the pellets are kept dry and intact. They also tend to be faithful to their roost so many pellets accumulate in one place. Tawny owls use a number of roosts which are often in exposed locations such as old trees. Therefore their pellets are often widely scattered and soon disappear. Short-eared owls live on open fields or moorland, often perching on prominent tree stumps or fence posts. Look around the base of these for their pellets. Herons, gulls, crows and birds of prey also take mammals but may tear their victims apart, often leaving the head (the most important identifying feature) and sometimes digesting the bones. Their pellets form a less complete record of their diet.

A six-figure grid reference of the owl pellet source should be recorded although a four-figure grid reference should be used to approximate the location where the prey was captured on distribution maps of the prey. It is not possible to assess the age of owl pellets, therefore, if you want to sample the contemporary mammal community collect the pellets on a regular (e.g. monthly) basis. Owl pellets should not be collected from nest sites without a licence to do so.

Fox droppings may be mistaken for owl pellets. Look for the twisted pointed ends on fox droppings compared with owl pellets which have rounded ends. Foxes also tend to chew their prey and break up the bones. Fox droppings often smell strongly whereas owl pellets do not.

OWL PELLET WITH MAMMAL REMAINS FROM A CLEANED PELLET
Fresh pellets are generally black, older ones are grey or disintegrated
by the action of clothes moth larvae.

Pellet analysis

It is easiest to concentrate on one pellet at a time. Either tease the pellet apart using tweezers or soak the pellet in warm, soapy water to soften the matted hair and dispel insect larvae. Separate out any skulls first as these are the easiest bits to identify, followed by the larger bones. Place the skulls and bones on a dark background and compare the skulls and then the teeth from the lower jaw with the key in Appendix 5. The identification process may be slow to start with but you will quickly learn the limited options. More details are given in The Mammal Society's booklet on identification of prey remains in owl pellets (Yalden 2009). Owl pellets can be collected in batches and sent to The Mammal Society for analysis and recording.

Field Note 6: The Mammal Society Owl Pellet Survey

This survey started in January 1993. By March 2003, 103,700 prey items had been recovered from more than 29,300 pellets, from 221 locations. Twenty small mammal species were identified, with field voles, wood mice and common shrews accounting for over 79% of the prey items.

Alistair Love (2004)

Cat kills

Cats can be a useful source of records depending on the hunting ability of the individual and on its hunting grounds. Any small mammals, up to the size of a young rabbit may be taken although common shrews, field voles, bank voles, wood mice and house mice are probably the most common captures, but harvest mice and water shrews are also caught. The drawback of using your cat as a sampling method is that it is hard to know exactly where the prey was caught. It is probably safest to give a four-figure grid reference on the recording form with the six-figure grid reference (where you retrieved the prey item) in brackets with an explanation.

Field Note 7: Recorded mammal cat kills

While I was living in Durham over a 10 year period, our cat successfully caught and brought to me the third and fourth records of the water shrew in the county. [Shame on it! – Ed.]

Rob Strachan (1995)

Parts of mammals

Considering how many wild mammals die each year it may seem surprising that we come across so few carcasses. The vast majority of wild mammals either hide themselves away to die and decay in nests or burrows, or, are eaten by carnivores and digested to an unrecognisable extent. Remains are also carried off by scavengers. Occasionally, however, a carcass is encountered where one needs to identify the remains. Where the carcass has decayed leaving only the skeleton for identification examine the teeth, skull and limbs.

Teeth

Prominent canines indicate the individual is a carnivore. The absence of canines, but with prominent incisors suggests the individual is a herbivore. The incisors are used to bite vegetation from the plant. They are replaced in the upper jaw by a horny plate in deer, cattle and sheep. There is usually a large gap between the incisors and the molars.

Herbivore teeth have crescents on their grinding surfaces; carnivore teeth are pointed unless worn smooth. Muntjac and male Chinese water deer, however, develop large canines or 'tusks' for fighting their rivals.

The skull

1. **The position of the eye sockets**
   Carnivores have forward pointing eyes to allow them to assess the distance of their prey effectively. Herbivores have eyes on the sides of the skull to allow predators to be detected by a wider field of view.
2. **The attachment of jaw muscles**
   It is possible to identify a mature badger skull by a distinctive ridge (the sagittal crest) running along the middle of the skull. This ridge provides attachment for the powerful jaw muscles. In adult badgers the lower jaw does not detach easily from the skull.

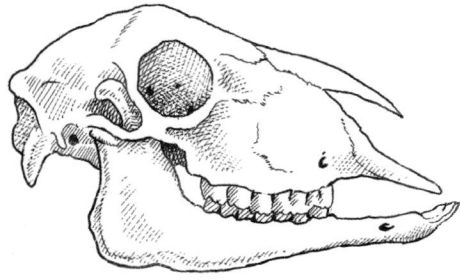

SHEEP SKULL – AN EXAMPLE OF A TYPICAL HERBIVORE. THERE IS NO SAGITTAL CREST, NO CANINES AND A BIG GAP BETWEEN THE FRONT INCISOR TEETH AND THE MOLARS AT THE BACK. SHEEP AND DEER HAVE NO INCISORS AT THE FRONT OF THE UPPER JAW.

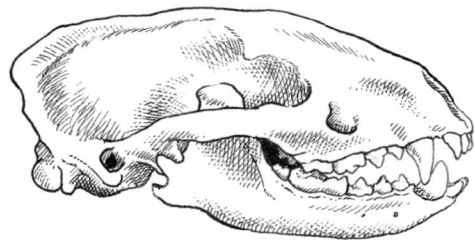

BADGER SKULL WITH PROMINENT SAGITTAL CREST. BADGERS ARE OMNIVOROUS AND THEIR CANINES AND MOLARS ARE BLUNTER THAN IN OTHER CARNIVORE SPECIES. NEVERTHELESS, THEIR TEETH FORM A CONTINUOUS ROW, TYPICAL OF CARNIVORES.

Antlers

Cast antlers can be identified from their shape (see Deer under Part 2 Making sightings). Cast antlers have often been chewed or nibbled by rodents.

Part 6 Live trapping

An obvious way of sampling the small mammals in an area is to catch and identify some of them alive. Small mammal trapping can be organised relatively easily but specialist licences must be obtained from the statutory agencies for trapping shrews, dormice and large mammals.

Small mammal trapping

Live trapping small mammals is a fascinating way to learn more about them and gives you the opportunity to observe the animals in the hand. However, it needs to be done with care and patience and can be time consuming. If trapping is being carried out as part of an exercise to estimate the population size or home range of small mammals refer to The Mammal Society's more detailed booklets, where further tips on trapping may be found.

Live trapping using Longworth traps and plastic 'Trip Traps'

Equipment: Traps (minimum of 20 for full survey of a site). Hay to provide bedding in the trap. Grain for bait and to feed trapped rodents. Insectivorous food for shrews must be supplied, such as dried mealworms or blowfly pupae ('casters') available from fishing shops. Flags (coloured tags on bamboo canes) to mark the site of each trap. A clear polythene bag in which to empty the trap and check for captures. Gloves for handling animals.

The standard and most widely used small mammal trap is the Longworth trap. This is composed of a tunnel, with a trip mechanism and trap door, and a nest box for food and bedding to keep captures alive. Longworth traps are expensive (from Penlon Ltd and major ecological suppliers) although members of The Mammal Society can borrow traps from the trap loan scheme. Plastic 'Trip Traps' can also be obtained from Penlon Ltd or pet shops (make sure you get one with a nest box). These traps are less robust and often less effective than Longworth traps, but they are considerably cheaper.

If shrews are likely to be caught, or if you deliberately want to catch them, a licence must be obtained from the relevant statutory agency (Natural England, Natural Resources Wales or Scottish Natural Heritage). Alternatively, contact The Mammal Society to obtain cover through The Mammal Society's block licence (covers members of The Mammal Society only).

Traps should be set in the evening so that captures are not incarcerated all day and all night and they should be visited at least twice a day, morning and evening, to check and release captures. With between 10 and 20 traps a range of species can be caught over a 3 day period. Spread the traps out (say 20m apart) and try to cover the range of habitats (e.g. woodland, woodland edge, grassland and wet areas) within a site. Mark the points to allow you to locate them again with a marked bamboo cane for example, or, to avoid drawing attention tie bundles of grass around overhanging branches.

Successful trapping depends on where and how the traps are set and the efficiency of the trapping mechanism of your particular traps. For a complete guide to Longworth trapping obtain The Mammal Society publication *Live Trapping Small Mammals: A Practical Guide* (Gurnell & Flowerdew 2006).

LONGWORTH TRAP (SHOULD BE COVERED WHEN SET)

Camera traps

Trail cameras can capture activity on still or video pictures, day and night. They detect the movement of an object (such as a mammal), passing across a background of a different temperature, using a passive infrared (PIR) sensor to trigger the device. The camera is positioned by an entrance hole, feeding station or animal path, on a post, tree or a tripod, and then checked or retrieved sometime later. There is often a small screen for setting up and for reviewing captured images. Housed in a waterproof casing, they can be light and portable with a very low drain on batteries, and are ideal for non-invasive observations. Pictures and videos are saved on to an SD card and downloaded to a computer using the USB lead generally supplied with the camera. There are a large number of stealth cameras on the market, some modestly priced, ranging from basic 3 megapixels to HD quality.

Nest boxes and nest tubes

Dormouse nest boxes

Dormouse boxes, similar to bird boxes but erected with the entrance hole facing a tree trunk, are one of the few ways of studying dormice. Their success depends on how and where they are positioned. You do not need a licence to set up boxes but you do need one as soon as you find a dormouse inside in order to examine it or check further nest boxes on site. You might also find wood mice, yellow-necked mice and other species in dormice boxes therefore it is advisable to wear gloves when checking the boxes. For further details obtain The Mammal Society publication *A Practical Guide to Dormouse Conservation* (Bright & Morris 1989) or see *The Dormouse Conservation Handbook*, available via the websites of the People's Trust for Endangered Species (PTES) or Natural England.

Dormouse nest tubes

These can be used in the same way as nest boxes to check for the presence of dormice. They consist of two parts, a wooden tray and plastic nesting tube. These tubes are much smaller and lighter than boxes and are especially useful in areas of non-traditional habitat such as hedgerows or areas of scrub. Nest tubes can be purchased from The Mammal Society. Again, licences are needed and more details on the use of nest tubes are available – see above.

Field Note 8: **Recording small mammals in nest boxes**

> The two largest yellow-necked mice ever recorded, weighing over 50g, were both caught in dormouse nest boxes.
> *Pat Morris*

Submitting mammal records

Records gathered in the field should generally be submitted online or by post to the Local Records Centre (LRC), ideally on a quarterly basis or as requested. This allows easier management of data and enables regular feedback such as newsletters to recorders. When mammal records are sent in to the LRC they are validated and verified (essential to ensure the accuracy of information collected) and digitized (entered into a database). The LRC is the most effective conduit for those gathering local records, supported by initiatives such as this guide and iSpot mentioned below, and provides the capacity to sensitively disseminate and use that information. LRCs are usually either dedicated organisations or based with the local authority or wildlife trust. County mammal recorders are also usually affiliated to them, as a volunteer or employee.

The data gathered from recorders is essential for protecting, enhancing and understanding our natural environment, as well as mammal populations, and in order to do this effectively we need good quality information. LRCs are able to support the recording community, both formal groups and individuals, providing secure facilities to store and manage records along with services such as website hosting.

Surrey Biodiversity Information Centre (SBIC), for example, works closely with the Surrey Mammal Group and regularly provides maps to assist them in gathering data. It provides training to develop recording skills as well as grants to assist groups with purchasing equipment. LRCs also organise events such as bioblitzes, which engage new audiences in recording, and provide an opportunity for knowledge exchange with more experienced recorders. LRCs will also hold other species records along with information on topography, habitat and landscape data. Correlating this data with mammal records can be helpful, for example highlighting potential sites where a particular species might occur and which would be worth surveying. For many counties the development of a mammal atlas is a key objective. LRCs can assist all stages of this process: from helping to target recording effort to areas that are less well surveyed and collating records as they are submitted, through to publication and sales.

LRCs also collate records from other wildlife trusts, local authorities, national wildlife organisations (e.g. The Mammal Society) and, when available, from commercial bodies such as ecological consultants. National survey and monitoring records, from The Mammal Society's Mini Mammal Monitoring Survey and the PTES's Mammals on Roads Survey for example, are often verified internally by in-house experts but made available to LRCs who can contact survey organisers if necessary. A free iPhone app (which records the location automatically by GPS) simplifies the collection and submission of records by motorists contributing to the PTES annual road survey of UK mammals.

LRCs share and upload data to the Biological Record Centre and National Biodiversity Network. The Biological Records Centre (**www.brc.ac.uk**) is the national focus for species recording, working with the voluntary recording community (local centres, etc.) across the country. The National Biodiversity Network (**www.nbn.org.uk**) hosts the NBN Gateway, a data 'warehouse' for biodiversity information, which can be quickly and easily accessed online, to help understand the distribution of particular species in the UK.

Obtain contact details for your LRC from the Association for Local Environmental Record Centres (ALERC) (**www.alerc.org.uk/**), the national body of all LRCs.

Sources of help confirming mammal records

Online help with mammal identification is also available (free) on the iSpot website (**www.iSpot.org.uk**), from The Open University. This site is designed to help people learn how to identify wildlife (including mammals but covering all groups), by putting novices in touch with experts. Launched in 2009, by 2012 iSpot had over 18,000 registered users, mostly people who have seen a species they don't recognise, or who have made an identification but want to check that it's the correct one. The replies come from a wide range of experts such as national recording scheme organisers, museum curators and from natural history societies. iSpot in turn helps to publicise the activities of the various schemes and societies, and data from the observations on the site can be passed on to the recording schemes. If you want to share what you have seen, need help with identifications, or would like to help others who may have less experience than you, then iSpot provides a meeting place that is open to all.

The Mammal Society and the PTES are represented on iSpot, and the details of mammal observations that have been confirmed on iSpot are shared with The Mammal Society, to be incorporated in the national database.

Summary

Mammal records can be collected in many ways. It requires patience, skill, knowledge and luck but this makes it all the more rewarding. This manual attempts to provide the mammal observer with the skill and knowledge needed to collect valuable mammal data which can be used for mammal conservation. The manual covers the range of methods which can be used, outlines the critical information needed to use each method and recommends further relevant sources of information where appropriate.

Mammal Index

Badger	2, 4, 5, 6, 7, 22, 24, 25, 28, 30, 33, 34, 36, 37, 38, 45, 51, 60, 62, 63, 70
Bank vole	4, 5, 8, 10, 11, 24, 35, 36, 46, 48, 50, 63, 67, 69
Black rat	4, 13, 27, 60, 62, 63
Brown hare	4, 5, 14, 24, 26, 32, 47, 63
Brown rat	4, 13, 24, 26, 31, 37, 63, 68, 69
Chinese water deer	4, 15, 17, 22, 24, 29, 30, 32, 51, 60, 62, 63
Common shrew	4, 7, 11, 22, 24, 26, 27, 46, 48, 50, 60, 61, 62, 63, 66, 69
Edible dormouse	4, 5, 12, 22, 24, 43, 60, 62, 63
Fallow deer	4, 5, 15, 17, 22, 24, 29, 32, 60, 62, 63
Field vole	2, 4, 10, 11, 24, 35, 44, 46, 50, 63, 67
Fox	4–7, 22, 24, 25, 27, 31, 34, 36, 38, 49, 63, 70
Goat	29, 30, 63
Grey squirrel	2, 4, 12, 22, 24, 26, 31, 35, 40, 60, 62, 63
Harvest mouse	4, 5, 8, 9, 11, 24, 41, 42, 46, 63, 68
Hazel dormouse	4, 5, 8, 9, 11, 12, 24, 35, 40, 41, 43, 46, 54, 60, 61, 62, 63, 68, 70
Hedgehog	4, 5, 6, 22, 24, 26, 31, 32, 40, 41, 43, 44, 47, 60, 62, 63, 70
House mouse	4, 8, 9, 11, 24, 31, 36, 46, 63, 68
Mink	2, 4, 6, 19, 20, 24, 28, 33, 39, 60, 62, 63
Mole	1, 4, 23, 24, 25, 36, 37, 63, 66
Mountain hare	3, 4, 5, 14, 24, 26, 32, 60, 62, 63
Muntjac	4, 15, 17, 22, 24, 29, 32, 60, 62, 63
Otter	4, 5, 20, 22, 24, 25, 28, 33, 34, 39, 47, 60, 62, 63
Pine marten	4, 19, 24, 28, 33, 39, 47, 60, 62, 63, 70
Polecat	4, 6, 19, 24, 28, 33, 47, 60, 61, 62, 63
Polecat-ferret	4, 19, 47
Pygmy shrew	1, 4, 7, 11, 22, 24, 26, 46, 48, 60, 61, 62, 63, 66, 69
Rabbit	2, 4, 14, 22, 24, 26, 30, 32, 36, 37, 38, 50, 51, 63
Red deer	2, 4, 5, 15, 16, 22, 23, 24, 29, 32, 60, 62, 63
Red squirrel	2, 4, 5, 12, 23, 24, 26, 31, 35, 40, 46, 60, 62, 63, 70
Roe deer	2, 4, 15, 17, 22, 24, 29, 32, 60, 62, 63
Sheep	23, 29, 30
Sika deer	4, 15, 16, 22, 24, 29, 32, 60, 62, 63
Stoat	3, 4, 6, 18, 19, 24, 28, 33, 36, 47, 63
Water shrew	4, 5, 7, 11, 22, 24, 26, 30, 31, 44, 46, 48, 49, 50, 60, 61, 62, 63, 66, 69
Water vole	2, 4, 5, 6, 13, 20, 24, 26, 31, 36, 37, 35, 57, 60, 62, 63, 67
Weasel	1, 4, 6, 18, 24, 28, 33, 36, 63
Wild boar	16, 24, 60, 62, 63, 70
Wildcat	4, 21, 22, 24, 31, 47, 60, 62, 63, 70
Wood mouse	4, 5, 8, 9, 11, 24, 26, 35, 36, 46, 48, 49, 63, 68
Yellow-necked mouse	4, 5, 8, 9, 11, 22, 24, 44, 46, 53, 63, 68

References and further reading

Arnold, H. (1994) *Atlas of British Mammals*. Institute of Terrestrial Ecology. HMSO, London. (out of print*)

Bang, P. & Dahlstrom, P. (2001) *Animal Tracks and Signs*. Oxford University Press, Oxford.

Bright, P. & Morris, P.A. (1989) *A Practical Guide to Dormouse Conservation*. Occasional Publication no. 11. The Mammal Society, London.

Brown, R.W., Lawrence, M.J. & Pope, J. (1992) *Animal Tracks, Trails and Signs*. Hamlyn, London. (out of print*)

Clark, M. (1983) *Mammal Watching*, new edition. Littlehampton Book Services, Littlehampton.

Corbet, G.B. & Harris, S. (eds) (1991) *The Handbook of British Mammals*, 3rd edn. Blackwell Scientific Publications, Oxford. (out of print*)

Cresswell, W.J., Birks, J.D.S., Dean, M., Pacheco, M., Trewhella, W.J., Wells, D. & Wray, S. (2012) *UK BAP Mammals Interim Guidance for Survey Methodologies, Impact Assessment and Mitigation*. The Mammal Society, Southampton.

Evans, P.G.H. (1995) *Guide to the Identification of Whales, Dolphins and Porpoises in European Seas*. Sea Watch Foundation Publication, Oxford.

Gurnell, J. & Flowerdew, J.R. (2006) *Live Trapping Small Mammals: A Practical Guide*. The Mammal Society, Southampton.

Harris, S. & Yalden, D.W. (2008) *Mammals of the British Isles: Handbook*, 4th edn. The Mammal Society, Southampton.

Jefferies, D.J., Morris, P.A. & Mulleneux, J.E. (1989) An enquiry into the changing status of the water vole *Arvicola terrestris* in Britain. *Mammal Review* 19, 111–131.

Mitchel-Jones, A.J., Amori, G., Bogdanowicz, W., Krystufek, B., Reijnders, P.J.H., Spitzenberger, F., Stubbe, M., Thissen, J.B.M., Vohralik, V. & Zima, J. (1999) *The Atlas Of European Mammals*. T & A D Poyser, London.

Morris, P.A. (Principal consultant) (2001) *Animals in Britain*. Nature Lover's Library, Readers Digest, London.

Morris, P.A. & Harper, J.F. (1965) The occurrence of small mammals in discarded bottles. *Proceedings of the Zoological Society of London* 145(11), 148–153.

Morris, P.A. and Wroot, S. (1987) *The Preparation of Mammal Skins for Scientific, Educational and Display Purposes*. The Mammal Society, London. (out of print*)

Stebbings, R.E., Yalden, D.W. & Herman, J. (2007) *Which Bat Is It?* The Mammal Society, London.

Strachan, R. (1995) *Mammal Detective*. Whittet Books, Weybridge.

Teerink, B.J. (2004) *Hair of West European Mammals: Atlas and Identification Key*. Cambridge University Press, Cambridge.

Yalden, D.W. (2009) *The Analysis of Owl Pellets*. The Mammal Society, Southampton.

Downloads

Bright, P., Morris, P. & Mitchell-Jones, A. English Nature. *The Dormouse Conservation Handbook*, 2nd edn. From PTES (**www.ptes.org.uk**) and Natural England (**www.naturalengland.org.uk**).

Other related publications can be found on the websites of relevant organisations such as The Mammal Society, People's Trust for Endangered Species and Natural England (see Appendix 7).

* Out of print but may be available at libraries.

Appendix 1 Health and safety

If you go out on your own, always ensure that someone knows where you are going and when you will be back. The following notes are for information only; they are not a complete First Aid Manual! Always take care to avoid problems and, whenever an incident occurs, seek qualified assistance as soon as possible.

Bites and stings

Bites and insect stings are rarely fatal but occasionally cause an allergic reaction. Symptoms include anxiety, eruption of red blotches on the skin, swelling of the face and neck, puffiness of the eyes, impaired breathing and rapid pulse. People exhibiting these symptoms should be taken to hospital immediately. If someone is bitten or stung the principal aim should be to reassure them and, if necessary, arrange for their removal to hospital.

In severe cases, the casualty should be kept as immobile as possible and the affected part kept below the level of the heart. Where possible a description of the animal that caused the problem should be given to those treating the patient.

Diseases which may affect mammal workers in the countryside

The following diseases can affect workers in the countryside. Please read this and take action as required. If you are handling small mammals or droppings you should be especially aware of these. Avoid these activities if you have open cuts and grazes, or wear surgical gloves, and always wash your hands with detergent afterwards.

Tetanus

All outside workers should be protected with a tetanus injection, and anyone carrying out conservation work should check with their doctor that they have an up-to-date tetanus jab.

Lyme disease

Lyme disease is a bacterial infection transmitted through the bite of ticks. These ticks are generally found attached to vegetation or various mammalian hosts, particularly sheep and deer. Cattle and dogs have also been known to be infected. Ticks are particularly active between April and October and during this period you must be aware of the possibility of picking up a tick from vegetation, both for yourself and for pets.

Prevention

- Wear long trousers tucked into socks.
- Wearing light-coloured clothing can help spot the ticks.
- Use insect repellent on your skin (DEET) or Permethrin on clothes.
- Check clothes for ticks regularly.
- Check for ticks when undressing as ticks can stay in clothing and skin folds for hours.
- Remove any ticks attached to you (or a companion animal), if possible, within 24 hours using tweezers or a tick-removal tool. Simple steps to remove ticks: (i) grasp the tick head parts as close to the skin as possible; and (ii) pull upwards firmly and steadily, without jerking or twisting (twisting is not recommended as this increases the chance of the mouthparts breaking off, thereby remaining in the skin and increasing the chance of a secondary localised infection). Don't squeeze or crush the tick's body as this could increase the risk of infection by prompting the tick to regurgitate saliva into the bite wound. After removal of the tick, apply an antiseptic to the bite site. Don't use petroleum jelly, liquid solutions, freeze or burn the tick. After the tick has been removed, continue to check the bite site over the subsequent month, looking for signs of increased redness or rash.
- Keep any removed ticks for identification purposes.

Diagnosis of Lyme disease and treatment

The symptoms of early stage Lyme disease may develop 3–30 days after being bitten by an infected tick. The rash develops at the site of the tick bite and is often described as looking like a bull's-eye on a dart board. The affected area of skin will be red and feel slightly raised to the touch. The size of the rash can range from between 2 and 30cm and in most people it expands over several days or weeks. More rarely, meningitis-like symptoms may occur, such as a stiff neck, difficulty in concentrating and general tiredness. If, after being bitten by a tick, you suffer from any of the above, see a doctor. Say that you have been bitten by a tick and may be infected with Lyme disease. Lyme disease can be treated with antibiotics, but the earlier it is diagnosed, the easier it is to treat.

Blue-green algal blooms

Blue-green algae occur naturally in many inland waters. In still water in the summer they can multiply quickly and turn the water green, blue-green or brown. During calm weather the algae may rise to the surface causing a scum to form. Toxins may also be released by the algae. In humans the illness resulting from swallowing or coming into contact with infected water may be severe, but there are no reports of long-term effects. Pets are more likely to suffer a severe illness, and death may result.

Prevention

- Avoid both algal scum and the water around it.
- In areas where scum is present make sure that pets are not allowed to approach the water, and in particular, ensure that they do not drink it.

Diagnosis and treatment

Illnesses resulting from algal blooms include skin rashes, eye irritation, vomiting, diarrhoea, fever and pains in muscles and joints. If you believe that you are affected because you show some of the above symptoms, contact your doctor immediately and explain that you may have come into contact with algal scum. Similarly, if you believe that your pet may be affected, contact a vet and to say that it may have come into contact with an algal bloom.

Leptospirosis

Leptospirosis in the UK occurs mainly in two types. One form is Weil's disease caused by leptospiral bacteria in the urine of various wild animals, particularly rats (from which the bacteria can pass into water systems). The second, the Hardjo form of leptospirosis, occurs in cattle and can be passed to humans. Cases of Weil's disease are very rare, but the infection can cause kidney failure and even death. For field workers the most likely source of it is from stagnant water which has been infected, or through careless handling of dead rats.

Prevention

- When in contact with stagnant water or soil that may have been contaminated, always wear boots and gloves.
- Cover all cuts and broken skin with waterproof plasters before and after work.
- Ensure that water does not get into the eyes, nose or mouth. Do not bite your nails.
- After working with or near dirty water, wash your hands and forearms with soap and water, particularly before eating, drinking or smoking. Equipment should also be rinsed and dried as soon as possible.
- Avoid contact with rat urine.

Diagnosis and treatment

Symptoms begin within 3–19 days of being exposed to the bacteria. Flu-like symptoms are common, including a high temperature and muscle pains. Other symptoms include conjunctivitis and jaundice.

If you suffer from any of the above symptoms and have possibly been exposed to Weil's disease, contact your doctor immediately. Explain that you may have been exposed to the disease and ask for an 'ELISA' blood test to check for the presence of the disease. Early diagnosis and treatment are vital for recovery.

For more information contact the Health and Safety Executive (**www.hse.gov.uk**) who run an information line and produce a leaflet on leptospirosis.

Appendix 2 Mammals and the Law

Anyone studying wild mammals ought to know something about the legal framework within which they are working. There are several pieces of legislation protecting mammals, or governing their management. The key points are covered by the Conservation of Habitats and Species Regulations 2010 and the Wildlife and Countryside Act (WCA) 1981. Various mammal species are protected by these pieces of legislation.

European Protected Species (EPS) – Conservation of Habitats and Species Regulations 2010

These Regulations enact European Directive 92/43/EEC, the 'Habitats Directive'. Specifically, **Regulations 40 to 43** provide protection for EPS, including defences.

- **Full protection** is granted to species listed under **Schedule 2**. These include otter, wildcat and hazel dormouse. It is illegal to catch, kill or possess any of these animals, or to disturb them. Note the definitions of disturbance are very specific, which is why these species still have some protection under the WCA.
- **Partial protection** is extended to species listed on **Schedule 4**. These include pine marten, polecat and mountain hare. These animals may not be taken or killed in certain ways as described in Regulation 43.

Protected mammal species – WCA

The WCA protects some other mammals extant in the UK. The relevant **sections** are **9**, **10** and **11**.

- **Full protection** is granted to some species listed under Schedule 5. These include red squirrel and water vole. It is illegal to catch, kill or possess any of these animals, or to disturb their places of shelter.
- **Partial protection** is granted to EPS species described above. It is an offence to disturb such an animal while occupying its place of shelter, or to obstruct access to said place of shelter.
- **Partial protection** is extended to species listed on Schedule 6. These include badger, otter, all dormice, hedgehog, polecat and all shrews. These animals may not be captured or killed by certain methods, except under licence.

Other relevant acts:

- **(Protection of) Badgers Act 1992:** Gives full protection to badgers and their setts.
- **Deer Act 1991:** Governs the management of deer.
- **The Wild Mammals (Protection) Act 1996:** Prohibits anyone deliberately mistreating a wild mammal.
- **Animal Welfare Act 2006:** Protects any wild animal that is under the control of man, i.e. an animal in a trap is under the control of man so becomes a protected animal and its welfare thus becomes a matter that is legally defined and protected. Cruelty or failure to look after the animal properly is illegal, as though it were a normal domestic species.

Non-native species

Section 14 of the WCA makes it an offence to release any animal that is not native to the UK (as defined in the Act). This includes a number of species that are already established in the wild in the UK; these are listed on Schedule 9. They include muntjac, mink, grey squirrel, edible dormouse and black rat. It may be possible to release these animals under licence and a licence may also be required to keep certain species (under different legislation) (e.g. grey squirrel, wild boar).

Licences

Licences that allow an authorised person to undertake **a normally prohibited activity, e.g. capture protected species** or **disturb** them are available from the Statutory Nature Conservation Organisations (SNCOs) (Natural England, Natural Resources Wales or Welsh Government and Scottish Natural Heritage). So it is illegal to trap polecats, but if you wish to do a survey of polecats by trapping, you will need to apply for a licence.

Class licences are issued by Natural England only (at time of writing) for a range of activities. For example, there is now a class licence for those who survey dormice for the National Dormouse Monitoring Programme (NDMP) in England. Unlike general licences, you need to register; if you hold a current licence for surveying dormice you will be automatically registered. If you do not, then you must register using the form on Natural England's website. There is no need for a licence if you do not suspect that dormice (or other protected species) might be present, but once you have confirmed their presence, further disturbance is illegal without a licence. Licences are free and usually run for one year. You are required to keep a record of how many animals are affected and submit the data to the NDMP.

General licences are issued for a range of activities, including the sale, exhibition and possession of protected species and the control of certain species that are, at times, in conflict with people's interests (e.g. damage to crops and the conservation of other species). The most important of these if working with mammals is the general licence to trap shrews.

If this activity is taking place in England the licence is available at:
www.naturalengland.org.uk/ourwork/regulation/wildlife/licences/

In Wales, there is no general licence for trapping shrews. However, Natural Resources Wales do issue several personal licences for shrew trapping each year, and also issue a licence to The Mammal Society to cover all their volunteers who carry out small mammal trapping in Wales.

In Scotland, Scottish National Heritage issue a licence available at:
www.snh.gov.uk/protecting-scotlands-nature/species-licensing/mammal-licensing/ shrew-vole/

As any small mammal trapping programme has the potential to capture shrews, you should download a copy of this licence and be aware of the conditions attached. The Mammal Society advises as a matter of best practice that anyone undertaking small mammal trapping, and thus likely to catch shrews, acts within the provisions of the licence. You must take certain precautions to prevent deaths of shrews. In particular the traps must be provided with blowfly pupae or dry dog food to sustain the shrews until they are released.

Obviously this is not a comprehensive account of the legislation, only a guide to key points. Further legislation covers cruelty and mistreatment, research, hunting and other mammal-related topics. More up-to-date information can be found on the websites of the SNCOs.

Furthermore, the full up-to-date text of any piece of legislation, including amendments, can be obtained from **www.legislation.gov.uk/**. We would recommend that you always refer to the relevant section of the relevant piece of legislation if in doubt!

Protected Mammal Species

Protected mammal	Habitat and Species Regulations 2010	Wildlife and Countryside Act 1981	Other relevant legislation
Wildcat	Schedule 2 – Full	Schedule 5, 6	
Red squirrel		Schedule 5, 6	
Otter	Schedule 2 – Full	Schedule 5, 6	
Hazel dormouse	Schedule 2 – Full	Schedule 5, 6	
Pine marten	Schedule 4 – Partial	Schedule 5, 6	
Water vole		Schedule 5	
Badger		Schedule 6	Protection of Badgers Act 1992
Hedgehog		Schedule 6	
Shrews		Schedule 6	
Polecat	Schedule 4 – Partial	Schedule 6	
Edible dormouse		Schedule 6	
Mountain hare	Schedule 4 – Partial		
Deer (all species)			Deer Act 1991

Mammals listed on Schedule 9 of the Wildlife and Countryside Act 1981 meaning that they cannot be released into the wild

Mammals	
Boar, Wild	*Sus scrofa*
Deer, Chinese Water	*Hydropotes inermis*
Deer Muntjac	*Muntiacus reevesi*
Deer Sika (including any hybrid)	*Cervus nippon*
Dormouse, Fat or Edible	*Glis glis*
Marmot, Prairie (or prairie dog)	*Cynomys* species
Mink, American	*Mustela vison*
Rat, Black	*Rattus rattus*
Squirrel, Grey	*Sciurus carolinensis*
Wallaby, Red-necked	*Macropus rufogriseus*

Further Information

The following websites have useful information about the legal issues surrounding wildlife in the UK.
www.defra.gov.uk/wildlife-countryside/

England: www.naturalengland.org.uk/ourwork/regulation/default.aspx
Wales: www.naturalresourceswales.gov.uk/legislation
Scotland: www.snh.gov.uk/protecting-scotlands-nature/protected-species/

Appendix 3 British mammal species list with Latin names

Rodents: Order *Rodentia*

Red squirrel *Sciurus vulgaris*
Grey squirrel *Sciurus carolinensis*
Hazel dormouse *Muscardinus avellanarius*
Edible dormouse *Glis glis*
Bank vole *Myodes glareolus*
Field vole *Microtus agrestis*
Orkney and Guernsey voles *Microtus arvalis*
Water vole *Arvicola amphibius*
Harvest mouse *Micromys minutus*
Wood mouse *Apodemus sylvaticus*
Yellow-necked mouse *Apodemus flavicollis*
House mouse *Mus domesticus*
Common (Brown) rat *Rattus norvegicus*
Ship (Black) rat *Rattus rattus*

Rabbits and Hares: Order *Lagomorpha*

Rabbit *Oryctolagus cuniculus*
Brown hare *Lepus europaeus*
Mountain/Irish hare *Lepus timidus*

Insectivores: Order *Erinaceomorpha* and *Soricomorpha*

Hedgehog *Erinaceus europaeus*
Mole *Talpa europaea*
Common shrew *Sorex araneus*
Pygmy shrew *Sorex minutus*
Water shrew *Neomys fodiens*

Carnivores: Order *Carnivora*

Feral cat *Felis catus*
Wildcat *Felis silvestris*
Fox *Vulpes vulpes*
Badger *Meles meles*
Otter *Lutra lutra*
Pine marten *Martes martes*
Stoat *Mustela erminea*
Weasel *Mustela nivalis*
Polecat *Mustela putorius*
American mink *Mustela vison*

Ungulates: Order *Perissodactyla* and *Artiodactyla*

Wild boar *Sus scrofa*
Reeves' muntjac *Muntiacus reevesi*
Red deer *Cervus elaphus*
Sika deer *Cervus nippon*
Fallow deer *Dama dama*
Roe deer *Capreolus capreolus*
Chinese water deer *Hydropotes inermis*
Sheep *Ovis aries*
Goat *Capra hircus*

Appendix 4 **How to read a grid reference**

A map of Great Britain is covered by 100km squares, each of which is identified by a set of two letters.

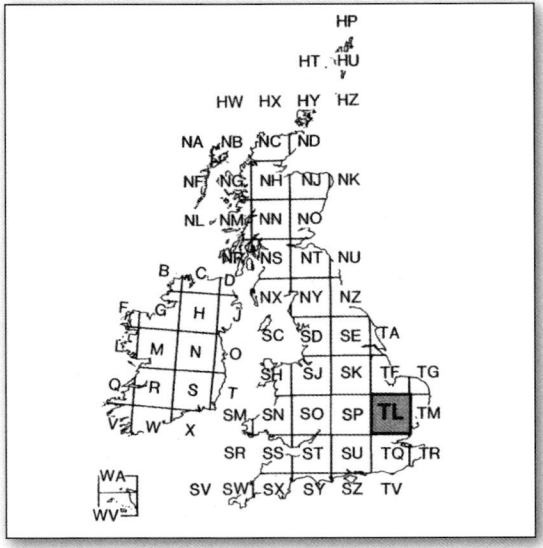

On Ordnance Survey maps these 100km squares are further subdivided into smaller squares by grid lines representing 10km spacing, each numbered from 0 to 9 in an easterly (left to right) and northerly (upwards) direction from the southwest corner.

Using this system you can identify the 1:25,000 maps of your area. For example, the shaded square below is TL 73 and so on.

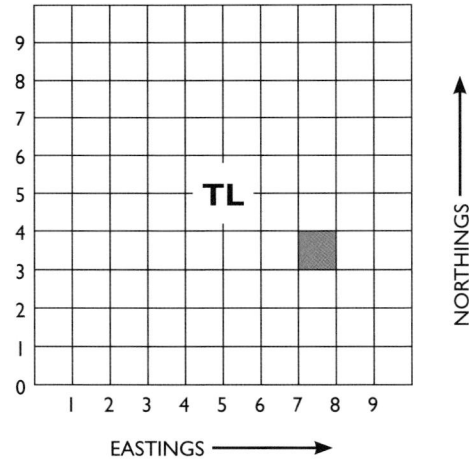

After the letters you quote the eastings first – then the northings. If you have trouble remembering, say 'along the hall then up the stairs' or easting and then northing (in alphabetical order).

On Ordnance Survey Landranger maps, you can find the two grid letters on the legend or on the corners of the map. The grid has also been further divided into 1km intervals.

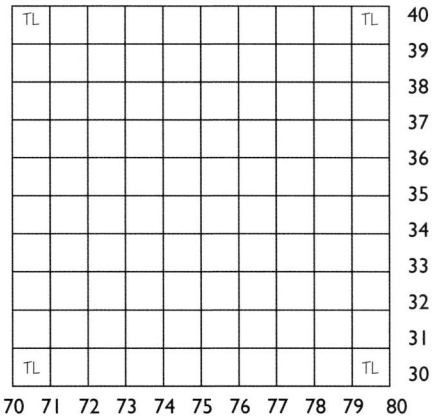

By estimating the eastings and northings to one-tenth of the grid interval you can specify a full six-figure map reference, accurate to within 100m on the ground. All you do is guess how many tenths away from the grid your point falls. Half way to the next grid is five-tenths – and so on. Quote all the eastings first, then the northings.

The 100m grid reference is shown like this: **TL 763317**; an example of a six-figure reference.

Here is a 1:50,000 Landranger map extract. Use the National Grid reference system to find:
The Church at **SK 568970**.

Modified from the Ordnance Survey leaflet:
HOW TO TAKE A GRID REFERENCE

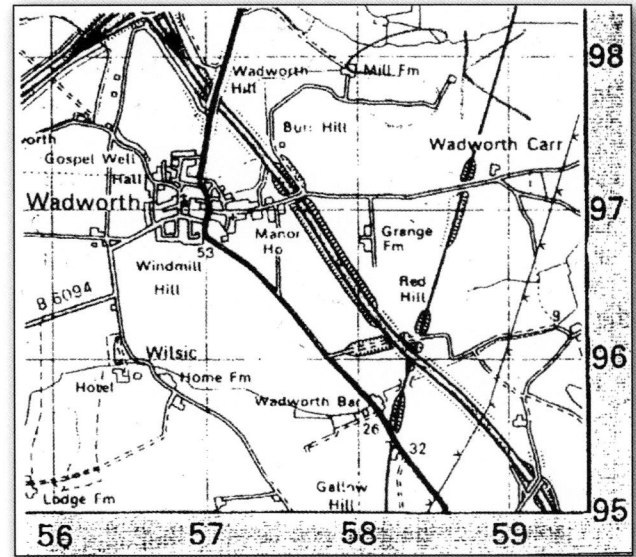

Appendix 5 Key to the identification of small mammal skulls

First, are you sure it is a small mammal skull? Note that amphibian skulls are very flat and have no teeth. Reptile skulls fall apart easily and are therefore found as fragments. Their teeth are minute, almost too small to see.

Bat, Insectivore or Rodent?

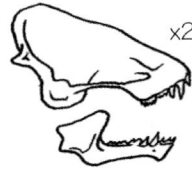

BAT (PIPISTRELLE)

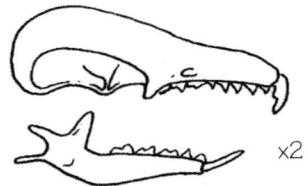

INSECTIVORE
SKULL LONG AND NARROW,
NO PROMINENT CHEEKBONES.
TEETH EVENLY SPACED
ALONG JAW

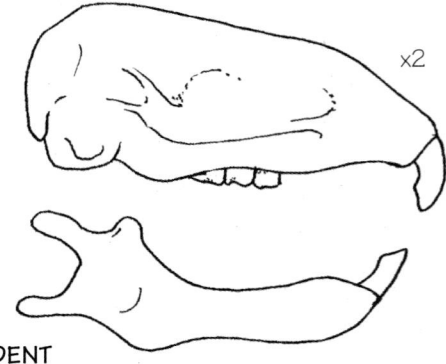

RODENT
SKULL BROAD WITH PROMINENT CHEEKBONES.
BIG GAP BETWEEN INCISORS AND CHEEK TEETH

A. Insectivores

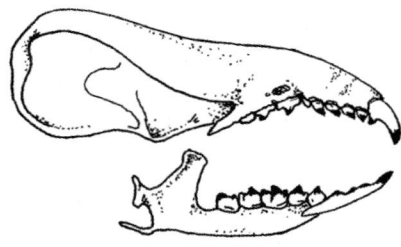

COMMON OR PYGMY SHREW

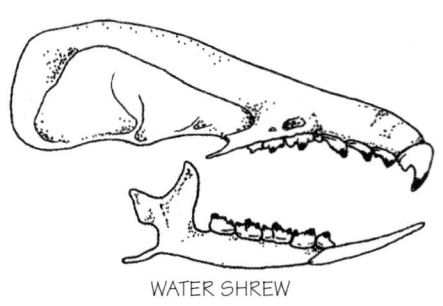

WATER SHREW

COMMON SHREW
SKULL (21 MM) _____
LOWER JAW (14 MM) _____

PYGMY SHREW (APPEARS VERY TINY)
SKULL (12 MM) _____
LOWER JAW (10 MM) _____

WATER SHREW
SKULL (22 MM) _____
LOWER JAW (16 MM) _____

SHREW TEETH ARE TIPPED WITH RED UNLESS BADLY WORN.

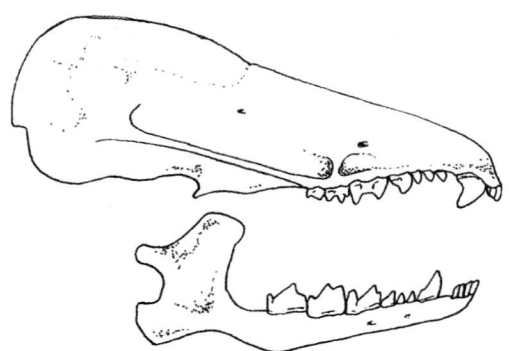

MOLE
VERY LARGE SKULL. TEETH ARE WHITE, LOWER INCISORS SMALL, NOT LONG BLADES AS IN SHREWS.

SKULL _____
(34 MM)
LOWER JAW _____
(23 MM)

B. Rodents

Voles can be distinguished from mice and rats by the shape of the tooth sockets. Pull out the front molar from the upper jaw and examine the hole left behind. Voles have a long jagged hole for all three teeth, mice and rats have separate holes for each of the three or four roots for each tooth.

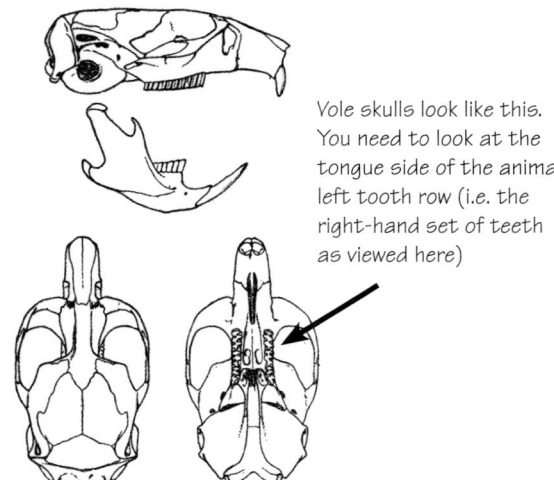

Vole skulls look like this. You need to look at the tongue side of the animal's left tooth row (i.e. the right-hand set of teeth as viewed here)

SKULL SIZES:

FIELD/BANK VOLE
SKULL (23 MM)
LOWER JAW (13 MM)
TOOTH ROW (9 MM)

WATER VOLE (MUCH LARGER)
SKULL (43 MM)
LOWER JAW (32 MM)
TOOTH ROW (12 MM)

Voles have zig-zag teeth

FIELD AND BANK VOLES ARE A SIMILAR SIZE BUT THEIR TEETH DIFFER.
LOOK AT THE UPPER TOOTH ROW ON THE ANIMAL'S LEFT SIDE.

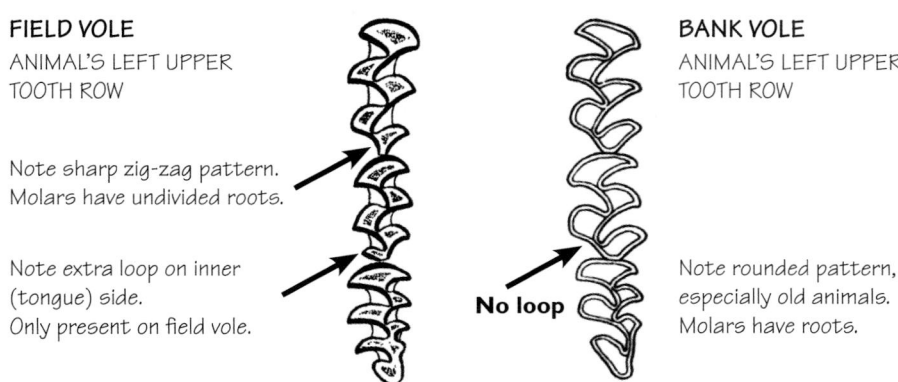

FIELD VOLE
ANIMAL'S LEFT UPPER TOOTH ROW

Note sharp zig-zag pattern. Molars have undivided roots.

Note extra loop on inner (tongue) side. Only present on field vole.

BANK VOLE
ANIMAL'S LEFT UPPER TOOTH ROW

No loop

Note rounded pattern, especially old animals. Molars have roots.

Vole teeth leave one long ragged socket when pulled out.

VOLE TEETH

BANK VOLE (MOLARS HAVE ROOTS)

 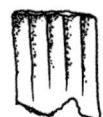 

Note young animals won't have developed roots yet

Roots developing

Old bank vole – molars have prominent roots

FIELD VOLE (MOLARS OPEN-ROOTED)
(Water vole is similar)
Molars grow throughout the life of the animal.

LOWER JAW

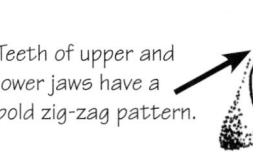

Empty socket with tooth removed

Teeth of upper and lower jaws have a bold zig-zag pattern.

Illustrations by A. Beer and J. Savery with guidance from A. Love

Mice and rats

Have knobbly teeth like humans teeth pulled out leave several holes for individual tooth roots.

Teeth have knobbly surfaces and separate roots.
There are three teeth in each of the upper and lower, left and right jaws.

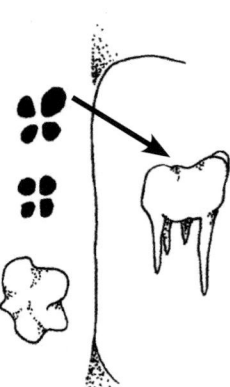

UPPER JAW
PULL OUT THE FIRST (FRONT) MOLAR AND COUNT ROOT HOLES.

LOWER JAW
SEEN FROM ABOVE
INCISORS AT FRONT, NOT SHOWN HERE

HOUSE MOUSE
THREE ROOTS
SKULL (24 MM)
LOWER JAW (15 MM)

WOOD MOUSE
FOUR ROOTS
SKULL (24 MM)
LOWER JAW (15 MM)

HARVEST MOUSE
FIVE ROOTS
SKULL (16 MM)
LOWER JAW (10 MM)

RAT
SKULL (36 MM)
LOWER JAW (25 MM)

HAZEL DORMOUSE
Four cheek teeth with several parallel transverse ridges.

Note: drawings are not to scale.

Appendix 6 How to identify water shrew faeces

Size Approximately 7mm x 2mm; when intact, noticeably larger than common shrew and pygmy shrew faeces.

Colour Dark brown/blackish when fresh (becoming paler when dry) with shiny fragments of exoskeleton.

Texture Granular, easily crumbled between fingers (in comparison, rodent faeces are tough and fibrous).

While the water shrew eats many terrestrial prey items it is the only small mammal to prey on aquatic invertebrates, which form the bulk of its diet. An easy way of detecting the presence of this shrew in aquatic habitats is to look for the presence of aquatic remains in its faeces. To do this, place droppings in a dish or saucer, add a few drops of water and gently crush to aid separation of fragments. Then carefully scan the dish using a binocular microscope (x50 magnification) for any aquatic prey items. Most common are remains of freshwater shrimps, water slaters and caddis larvae (see diagrams below). A mass of whitish, opaque or semi-transparent exoskeleton is also a clear indication of freshwater shrimp.

Diagrams of diagnostic prey remains

FRESHWATER SHRIMP – *Gammarus*

Two or three evenly sized and shaped segments followed by a relatively long and thin tarsus with a curved claw. These features are very indicative of a Gammarus leg.

WATER SLATER – *Asellus*

Highly variable and uneven segment shapes and sizes dependent on the function of the leg and its position along the body. Distinguishable from terrestrial isopods, such as woodlice, by the absence of large spines on the tarsi.

CADDIS FLY – various species
Very characteristically shaped legs. Some genera can be identified by a relatively long thin segment preceding a single straight claw, whereas others have distinctive double claws as shown.

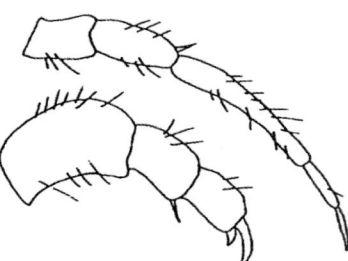

Listed below are references, providing detailed diagrams and additional notes, to help familiarisation with water shrew prey items.

Croft, P.S. (1986) *A Key to the Major Groups of British Freshwater Invertebrates*. AIDGAP 181. Reprinted from Field Studies 6 No. 3. Field Studies Council, Preston Montford. ISBN 1 85153 181 6.

Macan, T.T. (1974) *A Guide to Freshwater Invertebrate Animals*. Longman. ISBN 0 582 32275 X.

Tilling, S.M. (1987) *A Key to the Major Groups of British Terrestrial Invertebrates*. AIDGAP 187. Reprinted from Field Studies 6 No. 4. Field Studies Council, Preston Montford. ISBN 1 85153 187 5.

Appendix 7 Organisations with interests in mammal conservation

Badgers' Trust – **www.badger.org.uk**

Bat Conservation Trust – **www.bats.org.uk**

British Deer Society – **www.bds.org.uk**

British Hedgehog Preservation Society – **www.britishhedgehogs.org.uk**

BTO British Trust for Ornithology – **www.bto.org**

Deer UK – **www.deer-uk.com**

The Dormice Site – **www.dormice.org**

European Hedgehog Research Group – **www.ehrg.org**

The Fox Website – **www.thefoxwebsite.org**

Great Nut Hunt (PTES) – **www.ptes.org/moremammals/gnh**

iSpot website – **www.ispot.org.uk**

Joint Nature Conservation Committee – **www.jncc.gov.uk**

The Mammal Society – **www.mammal.org.uk**

National Biodiversity Network – **www.nbn.org.uk**

Natural England – **www.naturalengland.org.uk**

Natural Resources Wales – **www.naturalresourceswales.gov.uk**

NHBS Environment Bookstore – **www.nhbs.com**

People's Trust for Endangered Species (PTES) – **www.ptes.org.uk**

Pine Marten Site by the VWT – **www.pinemartens.info**

Red Squirrel Group UK – **www.snh.org.uk/ukredsquirrelgroup**

RSPB – **www.rspb.org.uk**

Scottish Natural Heritage – **www.snh.org.uk**

Scottish Wildcat Association – **www.scottishwildcats.co.uk**

Vincent Wildlife Trust (VWT) – **www.vwt.org.uk**

Wild About Britain (mammals) – **www.wildaboutbritain.co.uk/mammals**

Wild Boar in Britain – **www.britishwildboar.org.uk**

Wildlife Trusts of Great Britain – **www.wildlifetrusts.org**

Woodland Trust UK – **www.woodlandtrust.org.uk**

The Mammal Society is not involved in the management of these websites (apart from its own) and cannot be held responsible for the accuracy or condition of the content.

Form 1 **General mammal recording form**

NB: Each record MUST contain information under the headings in bold

Name			Address			Tel	
Date	**Grid Ref**		**Locality (or site name)**	Habitat*	**Species**	Abundance	Search method*
	2 letters	6 figures					
01/8/13	SP	435 205	1/4km SW of Grange Farm	J23 (Hedge)	Harvest mouse	1	XN (Nest)

Notes:
1. This record card has been completed and returned on the understanding that the information provided will be entered into a computer database and will be used for nature conservation, research and education.
2. * = Refer to The Mammal Society code card p.75 for codes and abbreviations.

Please return form to your County Mammal Recorder, or, if unknown to The Mammal Society.

Form 2 Site recording form

NB: Each record MUST contain information under the headings in bold

Grid Ref		Name		Address	Tel
2 letters	6 figures	Locality (or site name)			
SP	435 205	1/4km SW of Grange Farm		Habitat*	
				J23 (Hedge)	

Date	Species	Abundance	Search method*	Breeding status*	Activity*	Notes
01/8/13	Harvest mouse	1	XN (Nest)			

Notes:
1. This record card has been completed and returned on the understanding that the information provided will be entered into a computer database and will be used for nature conservation, research and education.
2. * = Refer to The Mammal Society code card p.75 for codes and abbreviations.
3. More than one code for Abundance, Search method and Breeding status can be used on each record.
Please return form to your County Mammal Recorder, or, if unknown to The Mammal Society.

Form 3 Owl pellet recording form

NB: Each record MUST contain information under the headings in bold

Species of owl												**Date** of collection			Sample no.	
Grid Ref (2 letters 6 figures)												Locality			**Name** of collector	
Habitat*												Site of roost				
				Prey species (give number of each)												
Pellet no.	Checked OK	Length mm	Breadth mm	Field vole	Bank vole	Wood mouse	Harvest mouse	House mouse	Brown rat	Common shrew	Pygmy shrew	Water shrew	Bird	Other	Min no. prey	
1																
2																
3																
4																
5																
6																
7																
8																
9																
10																
11																
12																
Min no.																

Notes:
1. This record card has been completed and returned on the understanding that the information provided will be entered into a computer database and will be used for nature conservation, research and education.
2. * = Refer to The Mammal Society code card p.75 for codes and abbreviations.

Please return form to your County Mammal Recorder, or, if unknown to The Mammal Society.

Form 4 Longworth trapping recording form

NB: Each record MUST contain information under the headings in bold

Grid Ref of line or grid		Day of session	**Date**
Total traps	Spacing		
Habitat*			
Weather since last trap round (delete as appropriate): clear/cloudy; day/night; wet/dry; hot/warm/mild/cold/below zero			
Describe location/position			
Observer's **name**			

Trap no.	**Species**	New or retrap	New no.	Sex m/f	Breeding condition*	Weight g	Notes
35	Woodmouse	R		F	GR	23	

Summary: Number captured by species for all traps (excluding recaptures)

Field vole	Bank vole	Yellow-necked mouse	Wood mouse	Harvest mouse	House mouse	Brown rat	Common shrew	Pygmy shrew	Water shrew	Other	Total

Notes:
1. This record card has been completed and returned on the understanding that the information provided will be entered into a computer database and will be used for nature conservation, research and education.
2. * = Refer to The Mammal Society code card p.75 for codes and abbreviations.
3. For further information refer to Gurnell & Flowerdew's (2006) *Live Trapping Small Mammals: A Practical Guide*, published by The Mammal Society.

Please return form to your County Mammal Recorder, or, if unknown to The Mammal Society.